S0-GQF-429

*The Literary Imagination of
Ultra-Orthodox Jewish Women*

The Literary Imagination of Ultra-Orthodox Jewish Women

An Assessment of a Writing Community

by ALYSE FISHER ROLLER

41039929

PS
153
J4
R65
1999

86 6/5/00

McFarland & Company, Inc., Publishers
Jefferson, North Carolina, and London

OHIO UNIVERSITY
WITHDRAWN
LIBRARY

British Library Cataloguing-in-Publication data are available

Library of Congress Cataloguing-in-Publication Data

Roller, Alyse Fisher, 1966–
    The literary imagination of ultra–Orthodox Jewish women : an
assessment of a writing community / by Alyse Fisher Roller.
       p. cm.
    Includes bibliographical references and index.
    ISBN 0-7864-0721-2 (library binding : 50# alkaline paper) ∞
    1. American literature — Jewish authors — History and criticism.
2. American literature — Women authors — History and criticism.
3. Orthodox Judaism — United States.   4. Women in Judaism.
5. Feminism — Religious aspects — Judaism.   I. Title.
PS153.J4R65   1999
810.9'9287'089924 — dc21   99-25985
                                       CIP

©1999 Alyse Fisher Roller. All rights reserved

*No part of this book may be reproduced or transmitted in any form or by
any means, electronic or mechanical, including photocopying or recording,
or by any information storage and retrieval system, without permission in
writing from the publisher.*

Manufactured in the United States of America

McFarland & Company, Inc., Publishers
  Box 611, Jefferson, North Carolina 28640

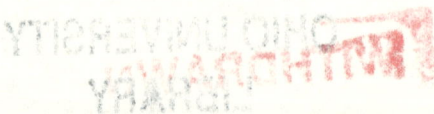

OHIO UNIVERSITY
LIBRARY

To Irving and Rochelle Fisher,
who give of themselves in many, many ways.

Acknowledgments

I would like to thank the outstanding faculty at the English department of the Hebrew University of Jerusalem. I am especially indebted to Professor Emily Budick whose generous encouragement and constructive comments were truly invaluable. I also thank Shira Wolosky, Shuli Barzilai and Menachem Blondheim who each made important comments at some point along the way.

I thank Chaya Rivkah Jessel for the generosity with which she shared her all-around know-how, good ideas and good spirit. Shira Schmidt made me aware of and provided me with helpful sources. I also greatly appreciate the time and effort Rabbi Yonasan Rosenblum spent in reviewing the manuscript.

My thanks also go to the following authors and publishers for giving me permission to quote from published works: Artscroll/Mesorah, Feldheim Publishers, Targum Press, Sarah Shapiro, Mindy Gross, and Michael Kaufman.

I thank my husband, Yosef Roller, for letting me tap his encyclopedic mind every now and then; it is like having a convenient fountain of Jewish knowledge in one's own home.

Contents

Preface

There is a growing awareness about the unique lifestyle of ultra-Orthodox Jews, who aim to fulfill every precept of Jewish law and custom. Sociologists, journalists and even novelists tell us how ultra-Orthodox men and women live. Daring research has attempted to understand how they think, their particular world view. It is largely due to this contemporary focus on the ultra-Orthodox Jewish community that its members have become more familiar to, and better understood by, the general public. Yet, even groundbreaking academic writing has proven that no researcher from the outside, no matter how well-meaning, can guarantee objectivity or sympathy in examining the ultra-Orthodox community. Researchers may claim to possess a healthy academic skepticism, all the while drawing conclusions that their research does not justify. The result is that they repress the very voices they have labored to disclose. Several potent examples of this type of research will be discussed later.

This study attempts to correct the outsider's bias prevalent in academic research by letting the literature of ultra-Orthodox Jewish women speak for itself while simultaneously expressing critical appreciation for its difference (to the extent that such a high-minded goal is possible). Ultra-Orthodox literature *is* the insider's voice and should be respected as a valid statement of ultra-Orthodox women's vision of themselves. Self-contradictions discovered in the literature should become evident as a result of close reading that is contextualized in ultra-Orthodox social reality, not in imagination or preconceived paradigms. This is no easy task, and only a fool would claim to have succeeded completely. None of us are immune to our own biases when reading, critically and otherwise. With the help of relevant criticism, we will see the ways in which ultra-Orthodox women writers tell us about themselves, about their affirmations, self-revelations and self-contradictions, about how they have been understood and perhaps misunderstood.

The literature of ultra–Orthodox Jewish women is not "high" literature. Its value lies less in literary finesse than in what and how it tells us about the cultural mindset in which it is written. This study, then, is a gesture of cultural poetics, a still fresh but established critical movement. It focuses on the English-language, nonacademic writing in the ultra–Orthodox Jewish world as a relatively new, spontaneous body of literature, an indigenous outgrowth of a different culture and outlook. This literature has grown exponentially in the past ten years, and the burgeoning of this body of writings testifies to the desire of ultra–Orthodox Jews to be heard in their own words, in their own literature. Yet this community speaks to itself. A universal feature of this literature is that it has remained largely unexposed to groups other than the ultra–Orthodox themselves. We can use this literature to get an unmediated view of how ultra–Orthodox Jews talk to one another, how they see themselves, how they see the world, how they use the creative medium of literature, how they use their imaginations. We will discover who these women are as well as what their literary contribution is.

Categorizing the human species by cultural and religious affiliations is not a scientific affair. The boundaries between associated groups are fluid, and no pat formulation provides a conclusive definition. The term "ultra–Orthodox" is objectionable on several grounds, mostly because the community to whom the term refers has expressed objection to it. Those proponents say that in observing the tenets of traditional Judaism they should be seen as and labeled "Orthodox." They argue that they represent the mainstream in traditional Jewish practice with nothing "ultra" about it — the "ultra" implying an unnecessary exaggeration in practice — while those who compromise the authentic tradition should have some prefix added. In popular reference, any degree of traditional Jewish observance, even minimal, is called "Orthodox" while the letter-of-the-law advocates are called "ultra–Orthodox" (or *kharedi* in Israel). In the end, I have kept the terminology, in spite of its faults, because it has become a part of popular usage and thus lends a clarity and uniformity to the meaning of the term.

For the purposes of this research, any writer is considered ultra–Orthodox if she consciously includes herself among those Jews who attempt to uphold every law and custom of traditional Judaism as it is presently practiced (whether she accepts the label "ultra–Orthodox" or not).

Another interesting feature of the popular, nonacademic prose of ultra–Orthodox Jews is that it is dominated by women as writers and readers. This creative literature is impelled and shaped by women. So, when we talk about the literature of ultra–Orthodox Jewish women, we are not talking about a minority body of writing within ultra–Orthodox literature as a whole but a major literary force shaping religious writing. These ultra–Orthodox women writers speak to ultra–Orthodox women readers and draw their subject matter from the women's life experiences. They seek to support and strengthen readers by talking about their own challenges, triumphs and conflicts as true-to-tradition women. They assume an understanding of the ultra–Orthodox lifestyle and its cultural presuppositions. Both in nonfiction and fiction, these women writers focus on women's spiritual, physical and moral heroism. Thus, in general, the literature is self-affirming, women-focused, and culturally self-focused.

Where *is* ultra–Orthodox women's literature? It is not normally found in public libraries. It is sold in Jewish bookstores which cater to ultra–Orthodox readers, and can be borrowed from one of the many book lovers in various ultra–Orthodox communities who open their often impressive private libraries for public consumption. This is popular practice in these communities. Such lending libraries in private homes are usually run by the woman of the house and visited by neighborhood women. They borrow the prose which is, as often as not, written by women. Thus, the dissemination of ultra–Orthodox women's writings is largely an informal, home-based, woman-to-woman enterprise. It also explains why it remains unaccessed by audiences outside of the ultra–Orthodox communities.

The readers of creative, non-academic writings written by ultra–Orthodox authors are mostly found in the various religious Jewish communities in the United States, Israel, England, South Africa and other English-speaking areas. The country of origin of most of those writers is the United States. Some writers hail from other English-speaking countries, and many have "made *aliyah*," or emigrated to

Israel. So, the United States and Israel are the two main centers from which ultra–Orthodox women's writing is produced and published.

In the framework of this study, I attempt to uncover the issues that ultra–Orthodox women's literature addresses, directly or indirectly. I try to place those issues in the context of traditional Judaism, Jewish feminist dialectics and feminist literary dialectics. I do so to ensure that each issue is viewed in light of its appropriate cultural or theoretical background and perspective.

This is an expansive, but not exhaustive, criticism of ultra–Orthodox women's writing. This body of literature is so unfamiliar in literary research that a main goal of this study is simply to introduce it to a critical audience. This study, then, should serve to open the discussion of ultra–Orthodox Jewish women's literature and its placement in critical dialogue.

Main Theses

This study argues three central theses:

1. Critical writing about ultra–Orthodox Jewish women consistently misrepresents or mis-analyzes that community, treating their voices as "other." Ultra-Orthodox Jewish women's literature provides a valid, untapped primary source for hearing them talk in their own voices.

This argument has been briefly discussed above. In addition to discussing the critical theory behind reading cultural and gender differences in literature, I will do a close reading of two well-known sociological studies to demonstrate the critical fallacies in academic research, which, I believe, fuel the creation of ultra–Orthodox women's literature in response.

2. The foundation of ultra–Orthodox women's literature is reactionary, a response to liberal feminist and Jewish feminist arguments. At the same time, authors sometimes promote or build on certain feminist ideals while nominally denouncing feminism.

Jewish feminism, in general, is an important conceptual framework to discuss because of its confrontation with traditional Judaism. Jewish feminism's challenge or reexamination of Judaism seems to be a reflection of Jewish feminists' identification as Jews. Yet the substance of their complaints against Judaism is also clearly inspired by the mainstream feminist agenda. As feminists, they find that there is no tolerable framework for the modern Jewish woman within Judaism. Their reexamination of Judaism consistently treats established ritual as a fluid, personal affair. Jewish feminists advocate adapting traditional rituals to suit feminist perceptions or creating new rituals in place of the old ones.

Ultra-Orthodox proponents view feminist attitudes toward Jewish practice as flippant in the extreme. In one response, Michael Kaufman — an outspoken advocate of ultra–Orthodoxy — emphasizes gender differences as the key to understanding the conflict between feminism and Judaism. He claims that mainstream (liberal or equal-opportunity) feminism affected the "masculinization of women"; that the goal of women's rights activism has been not the liberation of women but the emulation of men.

Judaism makes claims to women's difference, Kaufman asserts. The cultural role differences between men and women are not so much a function of social conditioning as they are a function of natural, psychological propensities, God-given differences. Liberal feminism's challenge of the whole idea of role divisions and gender differences was received by observant Jews as a challenge to a fundamental Jewish conviction. In the same vein, Kaufman recognizes that essentialist, or difference, feminisms pick up where liberal feminism parts ways with Judaism. This relationship will be discussed in the research.

Ultra-Orthodox women's literature is rife with examples of a subtle but persistent preoccupation with redressing feminist arguments and consciousness. The research will examine the terms of the literature's advocacy of traditional Judaism and the various ways in which it resists feminism.

The ultra–Orthodox authors' resistance to feminism is sometimes unsuccessful or contradictory: The writers nominally condemn feminist ideals while clearly utilizing feminist paradigms. They may couch their "anti-feminist" arguments in the terms of feminist thought, displaying a well-integrated feminist consciousness. In all types of nonfiction and fiction, ultra–Orthodox writers display a deeply assimilated feminist awareness, despite unconvincing disclaimers otherwise.

3. Two distinct voices emerge from ultra–Orthodox women's literature: the voice of baalot teshuva,* or newly observant women, and the voice of women from observant backgrounds. The former aligns with post-modern, feminist, self-reflecting narrative styles, and the latter aligns with traditional, masculine, universalizing narrative styles.

Within the general field of ultra–Orthodox women's writing, the *teshuva* movement deserves special mention. This is the growing movement of secularly raised Jews choosing to adopt traditional Jewish practice, usually sometime in young adulthood. Women authors who have taken on traditional Judaism constitute a direct link between secular feminism and the ultra–Orthodox community. Many of these women were self-proclaimed feminists or were deeply affected by Western feminist consciousness. Now prominent among ultra–Orthodox authors, their writings are characterized by both covert and overt defensiveness: They defend traditional Judaism against the internal voice of their ingrained feminist consciousness. Or, they may even defend feminist consciousness against its condemnation in traditional Jewish thought.

Baalot teshuva writers are often preoccupied with redefining their values so that they fall in line with Orthodoxy. They wish to refashion the way they think and act; thus they lend qualities of introspection, reexamination and personal yearning to the literature. The writers' defensiveness stems from the conflict between their feminist past and their traditional present, from their desire to reconcile internalized feminist values with newly adopted ultra–Orthodox values. The extent to which they succeed or fail will be discussed.

The narrative voice of the *baalot teshuva* is quite different from

---

*The term baalot teshuva *has religious significance in Judaism, and is popularly used to describe women who were raised in secular Jewish homes and became strictly observant as adults—who "returned" to traditional Jewish practice. The term* baalot teshuva *literally means "masters of return" in Hebrew.* Baalot *(feminine plural form) means owners or masters, and* teshuva *refers to any type of return, such as returning an answer to a question or "returning" in repentance from doing wrong. Of course in the case of* baalot teshuva, *the "return" that they are "masters" of is repentance. The term can appear in several forms:* baalei teshuva *is the masculine and generic plural form,* baal teshuva *is the singular masculine form, and* baalat teshuva *is the singular feminine form. Since the* teshuva *movement gained momentum in the 1970s, the number of secular Jews who have become religious reaches into the hundreds of thousands.*

the voice of ultra–Orthodox women writers raised in religious homes, who are typically more mature, having come of age before the *teshuva* movement and second-wave feminism ever started. The internal conflict of the *baalot teshuva* is nonexistent in the works of the "*frum* from birth" writers. The narrative voice imitates what Carolyn Heilbrun in *Writing a Woman's Life* called the "transcendent" voice typical of male autobiographical works. Indeed, the writing of non–*baalot teshuva* writers commonly displays an ungendered quality, a sense of the narrator's identification as Jew more than as woman.

These narrative qualities are most apparent in the Holocaust testimonials, which, by dint of historical incident, were written by older women from religious homes. Ultra-Orthodox women's Holocaust testimonials will be examined, therefore, to the extent that they conflict with or are similar to the voice in the personal narratives of *baalot teshuva* and in general women's Holocaust testimonials. They are also reviewed because they make a significant contribution to the literature of ultra–Orthodox women as a whole.

The Poetics of Difference

In looking at the literature of ultra–Orthodox Jewish women, we must first appropriate assumptions about femininity and the role of women in the context of traditional Judaism. The critic of ultra–Orthodox women writers must understand the unspoken assumptions of these writers and their audience. They are writing within a very specific cultural framework with specific presuppositions (such as pre-suppositions about the nature of femininity). One cannot simply read these texts as a feminist or social critic who is fluent in contemporary critical dialectics but illiterate in Jewish dialectics. One must become a cultural scholar of sorts, examining texts that emanate from a distinct cultural context. In looking at the texts, we are revealing the culture that produced them. If the cultural context is misunderstood, the text is misunderstood.

For example, a feminist critic might read a work by an ultra–Orthodox Jewish woman and determine it to be androcentric on the basis of its silence about women's concerns or its preoccupation with ungendered issues or issues that seem to apply to men alone. A more contextual reading, which would attempt to approach femininity from the author's own cultural authenticity, might determine that the writer's silence about women stems from the confidence of her position as a woman in the larger communal context. That is, her sense of empowerment as a fully participating member of the religious community gives her the freedom *not* to focus on women's issues. Of course the validity of this reading will stem from the text in question. On the other hand, texts that are dominated by gendered concerns might express a sense of the writer's insecurity or inferiority, her need to justify or apologize for the position of women. The point is that any social or literary evaluations of ultra–Orthodox women's writing must take into account the cultural presuppositions those evaluations challenge, the cultural presuppositions that the writer shares with her intended readers. Such an examination also necessarily becomes a lesson in that culture. In looking at the literature produced by a culture, we are profiling the culture itself.

Reading Gender/Culture Differences in Critical Theory

Elaine Showalter, in her essay "Feminist Criticism in the Wilderness," reviews and comments on the movement of feminist literary criticism away from revisionary readings of classical male-authored texts to a "sustained investigation of literature [written] by women."[1] Her essay is helpful in its sweeping scope of international feminist criticisms. Revisionary readings of male texts, she maintains, critique from the vantage of women as readers. Showalter points to this as the first stage in the evolution of feminist criticism. The drawback, she claims, is that revisionary readings remain male-focused. In resisting and challenging the artistic world view of a male author, they remain connected to masculine perspectives and cannot determine an essential femininity.

Showalter points to Patricia Meyer Spacks' 1975 book, *The Female Imagination*, as the turning point in the evolution of feminist criticism. Spacks' study remarked on the tendency of feminist critics up to that point to continue the stereotypical association of feminine imagination with inferiority by treating women writers less seriously. Included in Spacks' list are Simone de Beauvoir's *The Second Sex*, Mary Ellmann's *Thinking about Women* and Kate Millett's *Sexual Politics*.[2] Showalter points to Spacks' *The Female Imagination* as inaugurating a new era of feminist criticism in which the primary subject became the writings of women. Showalter writes:

> The second mode of feminist criticism engendered by this process is the study of women *as writers*, and its subjects are the history, styles, themes, genres, and structures of writing by women. ... No English term exists for such a specialized critical discourse, and so I have invented the term "gynocritics." ... It is no longer the ideological dilemma of reconciling revisionary pluralisms but the essential question of difference. How can we constitute women as a distinct literary group? What is *the difference* of women's writing?[3]

Showalter claims that the goal of focusing on women's writing is to free the feminist critic of an encumbering male orientation, allowing her to look at women as creators and determine what is essentially feminine in their literary production. The limitations of the quest to posit difference, which Showalter does not expound upon, is that our discoveries are still based on previous experience of masculinity in literary production. She rightly concludes that the culminating question will be one of essential difference, but even this question is still shackled by a male-centered orientation. To look at women writers in order to finally answer what is different about them is to compare women's production to men's. The question of difference is primarily asking, What is the difference of women from men? If we aim to determine what is different about women's writing, we are automatically using male writers as the starting point for the comparison and studying women writers from there. So, the question still remains whether even female critics are not presumptuous in their attempts to determine differences in women's writing that can be attributed to the writers' feminine difference and not, let's say, cultural difference. Showalter defines

> four models of difference: biological, linguistic, psychoanalytic, and cultural. Each is an effort to define and differentiate the qualities of the woman writer and the woman's text; each model also represents a school of gynocentric feminist criticism with its own favorite texts, styles, and methods.[4]

The first of these models, which is known as organic or biological criticism, is the most extreme positing of difference. According to this argument, literary femininity is actual, physical and innate just as a woman's body is the most basic, manifest femininity of a woman. There are extremist proponents of organicism, both French and American, who insist that the relationship between female writing and the female body goes beyond metaphor to the actual inscription of the female body in writing. Yet, in evaluating the success of difference feminism, whose goal is supposedly to define essential feminine qualities, biological criticism may be not only the most radical but may possess the most accurate paradigm of difference by not being obliged to differentiate between feminine and masculine artistry.

The most potent statement of difference is found in critical analysis that does not feel obliged to emulate the often constructed comparisons between women's and men's writing. Comparison as a methodology simply loses relevancy. The femininity of female writing is what it is, what we study and analyze it to be, just as a woman's body is the ultimate expression of manifest, essential femininity. To extend the biological metaphor, we *can* compare male and female bodies, but their respective masculinity and femininity is so incongruous, determined and independent that comparison is fruitless — or has us forcing neat dichotomies where those differences may be neither neat nor dichotomous. The literary analogy is clear. It is far more useful to delve into the depths of the author's work as a female writer and her own modes of expression.

While biological literary criticism holds potential as a methodology for defining an epistemological femininity, we still run the risks inherent in seeking out difference: that the feminine essence we define becomes the paradigm for a new stereotype, or that femininity is relegated to exotic romanticisms. We will examine current critical problematizing of essentialism more fully when discussing ultra–Orthodoxy's own assertions of essentialism. However, there is a fundamental premise of biological criticism that should not be ignored when looking at the literature of ultra–Orthodox Jewish women. The premise established by the body/writing metaphor implies that femininity is not acquired, taught or fully within our grasp of understanding. It is biological, inborn and in control of feminine imagination like menstruation and pregnancy are in control of feminine biology. The premise of the organic nature of the feminine imagination is a mystery. It is fundamentally like a religious belief, with its own set of not readily provable postulates and its mysterious, predetermined nature.

Here, the attraction of essentialism as a theoretical grounding in analyzing the writing of ultra–Orthodox Jewish women is clear. Both the artist and her critic follow the same feminist premise: The femininity of her expression is an inseparable part of her work. Her feminine imagination is supernaturally granted, inherent and different because of its incomparability to anything masculine. It is independent and speaks its own language. A critical discussion of her work is necessarily a statement of the female difference.[5]

It seems to me that the main goal of an essentialist school of criticism is to purify the focus on women authors. The goal is *not* to find how female expression differs from or is comparable to male expression but to establish the independence of the feminine imagination, just as traditional schools of criticism focused their attention on male authors and took the masculinity of their expression for granted. This is how difference-based criticism contributes to feminist theory: by postulating that femininity is unique, inherent and essential to female expression. Instead of seeking out the feminine difference in female expression, we will realize that by studying women authors, we are already looking at the feminine difference. The difference exists whether or not we can define it.

Assuming that the establishment of a feminine difference can conclusively move beyond conjecture, as many critics have attempted, the much-debated question still remains: *Why* are women different beyond the most basic of sex differences? Here the importance of cultural contextuality comes into play. Marian Lowe and Ruth Hubbard remind us in *Woman's Nature: Rationalizations of Inequality* that

> people are social organisms, and what counts is how we function in society. That depends on our opportunities and experiences, which are continually and inextricably affected by biological and social influences. The ways that we live are conditioned by the economic, political, and social institutions into which our biology is knit. We cannot sort them out and analyze what is "natural" about our social lives.[6]

What this means is that we may never be able to define a female nature. Therefore, we should be wary of relying on its stereotypes to build a critical reading. The turn in feminist literary criticism toward focusing on difference through the lenses of sex (biological) and gender (social) distinctions parallels feminist theory's turn toward establishing the paradigm of a constructed male/female gender dichotomy in social systems. Unlike early second-wave feminism's focus on equity and sameness between men and women, Showalter's demarcation parallels feminism's refocus on and celebration of women's difference from men, or what is widely termed "woman's experience," her ways of seeing and functioning in the world. That examination of cultural and epistemological difference feeds into postmodernist tendencies toward cultural relativism, toward a questioning of the reality and validity of objective points of reference and established categories, toward dispersing power sites and their truth systems in the Foucauldian sense. In this theoretical form, feminism focuses on cultural differences among women, as opposed to women's differences (from men) as a group. It seeks to culturally contextualize their experience and identity, to deconstruct the inclusive category of "women" because of what it excludes.[7]

Traditional Judaism is anti-postmodernism in that it believes in an objective point of reference, that at the foundation of all divergent renditions is *the* Rendition: the irrefutable word of God. Even here, however, in the last bastion of historical objectivism called Torah Judaism, there is a built-in postmodernist core (which sounds like an heretical assertion). All divergent renditions of the truth, which correlate to the various rabbinic debates in the Talmud (Oral Law), are considered to have validity. A multiplicity of interpretations seems contradictory from a human perspective, but Jewish thought tells us that each and every Torah teaching resounds with a myriad of interpretations, all true, all different. An iconoclastic coupling between the theoretical nucleus of postmodernism and the Oral Law demonstrates that the Torah system does not see an inherent antithesis between interpreting/deconstructing texts and objective truth. But while truth is a fluid and self-serving concept in postmodernism and cultural studies, it is an anchor and boundary in Talmudic "readings" based on the divinely granted Written Torah. No Judaic interpretation can be so fluid that it oversteps the Written Torah and the Oral Law as originally transcribed.

Thus, in both postmodernism and traditional Judaism, there is significant interpretive power in the hands of the reader, which leads us to a different type of literary criticism, namely reader-response criticism. Patrocinio Schweickart, in her essay "Reading Ourselves: Toward a Feminist Theory of Reading," comments on Showalter's argument in "Feminist Criticism in the Wilderness" by writing:

> If it is possible to formulate a basic conceptual framework for disclosing the "difference" of women's writing, surely it is no less possible to do so for women's reading. The same difference, be it linguistic, biological, psychological, or cultural, should apply in either case. In addition, what Showalter calls "gynocritics" is in fact constituted by feminist *criticism*— that is, *readings*— of female texts.[8]

By the activity of reading — whether as critic or not — the reader recuperates the text. Or we may say that the activity of the critic *is* the activity of the reader. Reader-response criticism tells us that it is the reader who gives meaning to the text — perhaps more than its author. Schweickart examines the spectrum of reader-response criticism and its varying opinions of who is in control of the text: author, reader or both. What we learn from Schweickart's discussion is that the reader's imagination must be taken into account as much as the author's imagination.

This is no easy task. Schweickart illustrates the invisible "ellipsis" in readings, which is the gap of cultural experience, whatever is "other" to the author.[9] Interestingly, Schweickart's illustration is taken from an address delivered to the Modern Language Association in which Malcolm X's writing is selectively recuperated by the speaker, a white male. Her point is clear: White male reading will necessarily include an ellipsis: African American male experience. It is not far-fetched to conclude that either a white, male critic cannot analyze an African-American male text, or that he must at least be culturally literate in African-American male experience.

Schweickart carries her point further:

> The feminist reader agrees with Stanley Fish that the production of the meaning of a text is mediated by the interpretive community in which the activity of reading is situated: the meaning of the text depends on the interpretive strategy one applies to it, and the choice of strategy is regulated (explicitly or implicitly) by the canons of acceptability that govern the interpretive community. However, unlike Fish, the feminist reader is also aware that the ruling interpretive communities are androcentric, and that this androcentricity is deeply etched in the strategies and modes of thought that have been introjected by all readers, women as well as men.[10]

If we follow Schweickart's point, we can conclude that male critics cannot help but read as males, and that means reading the masculinity of a text. It is questionable if women cannot help but read as males, due to the androcentricity of the "ruling interpretive communities." We can also postulate that just as a male critic cannot equitably read a male text that is culturally "other" to him, he certainly cannot be relied upon to read the femininity of a female text. By reading the femininity of a female text, I mean granting the difference (cultural, biological, linguistic or psychological) of the female author.

It also follows from Schweickart's premise that a female critic cannot justly evaluate the writings of women whose culture is "other" to her own. A Christian woman's critique of a Jewish woman author would contain Schweickart's ellipsis. That ellipsis, or gap, would be the experience of a Jewish woman. And what about the secular Jewish woman critic? Can she fairly criticize the work of an ultra–Orthodox Jewish woman?

These are the questions that must be asked in the wake of a postmodernist, multiculturalist consciousness. These are also the questions we can keep in mind when seeking to contextualize ultra–Orthodox women's writing: Can we properly read a text without appropriating the author's culture? Can we appropriate a culture? Can we appropriate the modes of thought and presuppositions that are internalized by the people who were raised in that culture? And without appropriating ultra–Orthodox sociopolitical culture, can we conclusively posit or judge its difference?

Chapter One

Critical Fallacies
and Jewish Feminism

The problem involved in criticizing the literature of a different culture is generated by the fear that we may squelch its literary voice. If we examine the literature of a culture that is foreign to our own — without due concern for discrepancies caused by cultural (or gender) differences — we may unknowingly misinterpret and obstruct a unique literary voice. Feminist and social critics are theoretically sensitive to the possibility of misreading caused by ignoring or repressing the context of cultural individuality in literary expression. Still, blatant critical fallacies occur when those who would champion freedom of expression for all distinct literary groups cannot live up to their own call.

Feminist revisionary readings are an example of the attempt to reveal the ellipsis in former critical readings, to lay bare the elusive gaps of gender discrepancies, to disclose the misinterpretation of femininity. There are many instances of this type of feminist criticism. Yet, how often does feminist criticism squelch literary voices which are "other" to its own?

Elizabeth Spelman in *Inessential Woman: Problems of Exclusion in Feminist Thought* explores the ways in which popular feminist criticism has subtly extended the privilege of a certain group of women who are culturally and economically dominant, namely white, middle-class women. She writes that criticism of sexist male theories has often served to blind feminists to their own perpetuation of privilege. Spelman writes:

> Our distancing ourselves from the vies of blatant sexists keeps us
> from recognizing the extent to which we may in fact share elements

of their views. It is always easier to see how privilege works in others than in ourselves, but the insights so gained may be entirely lost if we can't imagine that we are anything like those others.[11]

Spelman claims that self-blinding in feminist thought has usually taken the form of universalization about women's condition. The determination *not* to see the differences among women — the differences generated by classism, racism, anti–Semitism or any other form of oppression — has led mainstream feminism to endorse critical fallacies. Concerns that are prominent for one group of women may not be prominent for another. Observations that may be true for one group of women may not be true for another.

Spelman's line of argument against universalizing feminism is useful in warning us about the ways in which critical reasoning can be self-contradictory and can endorse the very forms it condemns. Her analysis reminds us that a compelling argument may still be based on ambiguous or incorrect assumptions, which is the first step in subtle oppression. The perception by ultra–Orthodox Jews of this exact ideological unfolding in feminism is relevant to our discussion of ultra–Orthodox women's literature. For the purposes of this study, I would like to focus on the arguments that mainstream Jewish feminism has launched against ultra–Orthodox Judaism. It is important to describe the effect of Jewish feminist criticism on traditional Judaism because the bulk of ultra–Orthodox women's writing was produced after Jewish feminism's criticism of ultra–Orthodoxy was widely known and felt. It is important to place this burgeoning genre in the context of the expectations of ultra–Orthodox Jews that it would counteract Jewish feminism. The literature produced by ultra–Orthodox women, most of which has been written since the late 1980s, can be seen as a spontaneous, if not conscious, response to the growing influence of Jewish feminism, which is viewed as a threat to traditional Jewish practice and values.

It is beyond the scope and purpose of this study to determine the full extent of the critical fallacies that came into the offensive and defensive plays between Jewish feminism and ultra–Orthodoxy. We will review several books that do just this. What we need to understand is that ultra–Orthodox commentators saw critical fallacies, foul play or simple ignorance in the feminist arguments launched against them and that they responded in various ways. Ultra-Orthodox women's literature is one response, the women's response; they created a writing movement that went far beyond the original, perhaps unrecognized, motive of resisting or reconciling feminist consciousness in ultra–Orthodox women's lives. We will see the ultra–Orthodox difficulties with feminism played out in the women's literature.

When we look at the early Jewish feminist criticism that arose from a multifaceted, boisterous women's movement, we often see a sincere grappling with Jewish issues. Ultra-Orthodox Jews may not have doubted the sincerity of Jewish feminists, but they did doubt their Jewish commitment. They considered Jewish feminists to be secular Jews, ignorant of Judaism for the most part but well versed in feminist ideologies. The feeling was that feminists wielded these ideologies injudiciously to serve the women's movement that nurtured them. Ultra-Orthodox Jews felt attacked, but they might not have responded if feminist arguments weren't so compelling or invasive into the ultra–Orthodox community itself. Formal ultra–Orthodox redress to feminist arguments has not been frequent, but it has been thorough. This leads to the conclusion that feminist arguments were taken seriously, even where it was argued that feminist platforms were based on half-truths or ignorance.

There may have been fear of the damage that might be caused by articulate Jewish women who are not committed to working within the bounds of Jewish law airing grievances that may ring true. There was also a feeling that Jewish feminist grievances were unreasonable, criticizing traditional Judaism for what was often not a product of its law but of the social norms prevailing at the time. In this light, it seems plausible that if feminist critique had been committed to the Jewish legal framework, which is seen as the essence of Torah observancy, and had focused its censure on aspects that could have been subject to change, then perhaps ultra–Orthodoxy would have been more accepting of Jewish feminist grievances, instead of resistant. The result of the disregard for Jewish law is that even Jewish feminist efforts that respected Jewish law and were committed to pushing for change within legal stipulations were often dismissed by ultra–Orthodox Jews, by the men *and* the women and their leaders, as a continuation of the same Jewish feminist agenda of subversion.[12] Jewish feminism simply had gotten a bad reputation among the ultra–Orthodox.

Religious scholar and writer Norman Lamm aired his assessment of Jewish feminism's disparagement of Judaism in 1978 in his foreword to Moshe Meiselman's *Jewish Woman in Jewish Law*, a volume that Lamm edited. Lamm viewed the book as a decisive response to Jewish feminism: "the first full treatment of the subject by a staunch advocate of the Jewish tradition."[13] His summation of Jewish feminism's effect is instructive to our understanding of ultra–Orthodox perceptions:

> The critique of Judaism — specifically, of the role of Jewish women in Jewish law — has frequently been more hysterical than historical, more apoplectic than apodictic. The millennial Jewish concern for the protection of women's welfare and dignity in a world where these were not at all taken for granted, was simply ignored or, worse, stood on its head. Nothing that the Jewish tradition had to say about women, it seemed, could be right ... and there was no opening for rational discourse and analysis.[14]

Religious writer and critic Michael Kaufman also describes the widespread influence of Jewish feminism and its assault on traditional Judaism:

> Jewish women began to be aware of feminist concerns during the [equal-opportunity/liberal feminist] period of the feminist movement. The confrontation between Judaism and the feminism of that time was as grievous as it was inevitable. It produced a huge amount of literature, nearly all of which was written by Jewish feminists expressing grievances against Judaism. The condemnations were initiated by women who were estranged from Judaism, but they were soon transmitted to traditional Jewish women as well, some of whom took up the call to arms. The new Jewish feminist claimed that Judaism's "patriarchal" society kept women in a second-class status similar to, or worse than, the conditions under which women had suffered throughout the ancient world. Some blamed "patriarchal Judaism" for women's oppression throughout the Western world.[15]

As a traditional Jewish scholar and writer, Kaufman's use of terms such as "confrontation," "grievances," "condemnations" and "call to arms" are indicative of ultra–Orthodoxy's impression that it came under ideological attack. Just as his work is a direct response to Jewish feminism, late in coming and singular as it is, the literature of ultra–Orthodox women as a whole is also a late, though less deliberate, response. This literature is a rejoinder to Jewish feminism, although it does not ideologically oppose it on all counts. The response is rather a different brand of feminism, meant to empower women in a different way, within the stipulations of traditional Judaism.

Early Jewish Feminism

It seems that mainstream Jewish feminism has not been interested in the expression of ultra–Orthodox Jewish women writers. There is little evidence that Jewish feminists read the writings that are examined in this book. For that matter, there is little evidence of feminist/ultra–Orthodox interaction altogether. Jewish feminists have been nurtured by the feminist movement and seem to identify as feminists first. The turn to Jewish issues is not usually from within Judaism but from within feminism. This is evident in Jewish feminist writings in which mainstream feminist dialectics can be traced. In identifying more with feminism, in general, Jewish feminists have not developed any significant dialogue with ultra–Orthodox women.

It is also plausible to assume that ultra–Orthodox Jewish women and writers were never taken seriously by feminists. They were seen as the submissive products of androcentric subjugation. The result is that Jewish feminists have impelled many changes in the way Jews practice and regard Judaism. But from the religious point of view, the result has been the subversion of Jewish tradition. Kaufman describes the disruptive effect of mainstream Jewish feminism on female Jewish solidarity:

> Jewish feminists were viewed by traditionalists as traitors who had forsaken Judaism. Orthodox women who expressed understanding for feminist concerns found themselves estranged from their observant sisters. Conversely, women who remained loyal to Jewish tradition, marrying and raising families, were derided by their "liberated" sisters as "breeders," harem wives, female Uncle Toms, "Tante Tovahs." Men and women who had the temerity to defend Jewish tradition were dismissed as apologists by feminist polemicists.[16]

Early Jewish feminism in general categorically resisted or rejected ultra–Orthodoxy, especially under the influence of radical feminism, which follows the example of a postmodern cynicism toward established power/truth sites in the Foucauldian sense. Critical fallacies came into play when Jewish feminism reinterpreted Jewish traditions and then, upon subverted premises, built newer ones.

In order to understand the political/religious adversity to ultra–Orthodoxy by mainstream Jewish feminism, we can look at some of the critical literature that Jewish feminism has produced. This will give us some of the cultural appropriation we desire, that is, an appreciation of the cultural atmosphere in which ultra–Orthodox women's literature is written, an illustration of the feminist ideas that engendered (in the old-fashioned sense of the word) ultra–Orthodox resistance. This resistance, in turn, molded the reactionary core of ultra–Orthodox women's writing.

One of the most outstanding features of mainstream Jewish feminism is the inherent ambivalence of its position. On one hand, many Jewish feminists strongly identify as Jews and feel a strong commitment to the Jewish community. On the other hand, they find that, as feminists, there is no satisfactory framework for the modern Jewish woman in traditional Judaism; that it is necessary to forge a new framework. Theirs, in short, is a love/hate relationship with traditional Judaism. An early anthology of Jewish feminism, *Jewish Woman: New Perspectives*, strongly reflects this ambivalence and is introduced as such:

> While some [contributing writers] focus on progress already made, most attempt reexaminations of Jewish history, culture, law, ritual, and communal organization in an attempt to understand more clearly both how the community has been structured in the past, and what changes might be possible for the future. All question traditional sex-role differentiation within Judaism while maintaining strong commitment to Jewish tradition and survival. The tension between these two perspectives provides the framework for this anthology.[17]

Reexamination, rereading history, is a critical activity that first began in the women's movement, then found its way into mainstream Jewish feminism and, later, as we will see, into ultra–Orthodox Jewish criticism. In mainstream Jewish feminism, however, this reexamination reflects ambivalence and tension and takes two turns. It will either partially affirm traditional Jewish practice and interpretation — or subvert it. And what is more important to our discussion is that ultra–Orthodoxy perceives feminism's ambivalent treatment of traditional Judaism as misdirected subversion and disloyalty.

Blu Greenberg is the traditionalist of *Jewish Woman: New Perspectives*. She asserts the value of Jewish rabbinic tradition yet calls for reinterpretation. She wants to see changes made within the framework of existing Jewish law: Laws based on realities that she deems no longer relevant should be modified. On the whole she calls for reconciliation between Judaism and feminism.

> What is sorely needed today is the creation of a dialectical tension between Jewish values and the mores of modern society in light of the far-reaching implications of Women's Liberation. One crucial part of the dialectic would be to measure the halakhic and religious status of Jewish women by the feminist notion of equality of women. But there must be a two-way relationship of communication and influence instead of withdrawal and widening of the gap. Thus, an authentic Jewish women's movement would seek to find new approaches within *halakha* to respond to and express women's concerns. Simultaneously, it would seek to imbue women's concerns with Jewish values.[18]

On one hand, Greenberg believes that Jewish standards should be measured by the "feminist notion of equality of women," which means that feminism is the gauge by which Judaism must be evaluated. Yet she also asserts that "since we are Jews, we need not buy the whole package of feminism. Rather, we must infuse a changing society with our own values and check the excesses to which all revolutionary movements fall prey."[19] One of those "excesses" is feminism's attack on the institution of the family as the berth of women's abuse, she claims.

While a traditional Jewish woman theoretically affirming traditional Judaism, Greenberg actually performs the same critical dissection of Judaism that most Jewish feminists perform, i.e., an ambivalent partial affirmation that makes the subversion of certain elements of Jewish law seem like an act of loyalty.

Other tradition-focused Jewish feminists grapple with Jewish issues and may be almost surprised, if not apologetic, if and when their conclusions affirm Jewish interpretations. Phyllis Trible looks at patriarchal subjugation in the Bible and concludes that it does not reflect the subjugation of women she perceives in the religions that developed out of it, meaning Judaism and Christianity. (She glibly throws Christianity and Judaism into the same pot.) She responds to those feminists who would condemn the Bible itself as sexist and not the religions that have been derived from it.

> The women's movement errs when it dismisses the Bible as inconsequential or condemns it as enslaving. In rejecting Scripture women ironically accept male chauvinistic interpretations and thereby capitulate to the very view they are protesting. But there is another way: to reread (not rewrite) the Bible without the blinders of Israelite men or of Paul, Barth, Bonhoeffer, and a host of others. The hermeneutical challenge is to translate Biblical faith without sexism.[20]

Trible doesn't see the need to differentiate between the historic subjugation of women in Christianity and Judaism. It's all the same thing to her: male interpretations determining patriarchal reality. Yet, she also uses ancient Jewish (male) sources to affirm her rereading of the Bible. Trible's essay gives the illusion of being committed to Jewish tradition. But she is actually making a two-handed movement: She completely undermines Orthodox Jewish tenets and practices while partially affirming their most fundamental foundation, the Bible. She does this by claiming that the Bible has value but that it must be reinterpreted. Trible's position is full of Jewish feminism's ambivalent embrace of traditional Judaism, seeking to challenge and change, or challenge while partially affirming.

Much of the rest of *Jewish Woman: New Perspectives* places the Jewish feminist agenda on its well-worn track of advocating the eradication of rituals, which have often been depreciated or misconstrued by critics, or the creation of new rituals. A major concern is appropriating old rituals and adapting them (which is relatively conservative) or totally subverting them (which is more extreme). The end result is that feminist criticism on the conceptual level is placed alongside practical suggestions to alter rituals. Where honest criticism may have been heard by the ultra–Orthodox were it committed to the framework of Jewish law, the subversion of Jewish ritual made that unthinkable. Ultra-Orthodox Jews were resistant rather than compliant to feminist ideas largely because feminists did not feel compelled to make changes *within* Jewish law, not to mention their frequently blatant ignorance about traditional Judaism and their charges of chauvinism based on misunderstandings of Jewish practice.

The irony of the concern with Jewish ritual by Jewish feminists is that it is taken up from the feminist point of view, not because of religiosity. As the opening article of *Jewish Woman: New Perspectives* states, "We are here because a secular movement for the liberation of women has made it imperative that we raise certain Jewish issues now, because we will not let ourselves be defined as Jewish women in ways in which we cannot allow ourselves to be defined as women."[21] *Jewish and Female*, an all-encompassing "sourcebook" (as it is dubbed) on Jewish feminism, expresses the same sort of wide-ranging attitudes toward Judaism, including the same preoccupation with appropriating traditional Jewish ritual as a feminist, which often means subverting specifically male-dominated rituals. A real engagement and concern with Judaism is evident, as is a disregard for ensconced Jewish legal codes. *Lilith* magazine, the fruit of Jewish feminist labors, is also allegiant to this ambition. The editors of *Lilith* dub it "The Prepared Table," explaining that this epithet, a translation of *Shulkhan Arukh*, the authoritative code of Jewish law, reflects the vision of their publication as a valid substitute for traditional Jewish observancy: "As Jewish feminists continue to rediscover and rework Jewish practice, the contents of *Lilith* may serve as an envolving [*sic*] Prepared Table for a new code of behavior."[22]

An article by a Reform rabbi, Elyse M. Goldstein, is a radical example of the shape that "reworking" Jewish rituals may take. She opens her article with her and her four women friends "splashing around with glee" in the *mikvah* the night before her marriage.[23] Her cynicism toward the intentions of male rabbis and rabbinic tradition is trenchant, as is her misunderstanding of Jewish law in the several instances that she reiterates it. And the intention of this inaccurate reiteration is to show how outlandish the traditions are, or demeaning to women.

Goldstein writes, "I dipped and sang out the traditional blessing, not meekly and with arms covering my breasts as the attendant would have liked, but in a clear, loud song."[24] There are many presumptions included in this quote. Some are stated clearly in the body of her article, and some are implied. She immerses in the *mikvah* and recites a blessing — and not just her own blessing but the traditional blessing. That is, she chooses to follow rabbinic tradition even as she shuns it. But not only does she shun the male rabbis who have interpreted the tradition, but she also shuns the women who have followed it, such as the observant *mikvah* attendant, who makes herself subservient to the terms of patriarchal ritual and also expects other women to do so — "meekly." Goldstein will follow the tradition boldly while she assumes that other women — nonfeminist, ultra–Orthodox women — do so meekly. She mentions the existence of ancient *mikvaot* (plural form of *mikvah*) on the top of Masada in Israel, that ritual immersion is a part of Jewish history and her own heritage. The women of the past who used these *mikvaot* supposedly did not do so meekly, even as they followed rabbinic interpretations of the law, which is the romantic model she takes for herself. However, contemporary ultra–Orthodox women, following the exact same tradition, do so meekly and expect meekness from other women, she implies.

As we draw out the meaning of the next phrase in the above quote, one reels from Goldstein's presumption and inaccuracy. She claims that the observant attendant would have liked Goldstein to have recited the traditional blessing not only meekly but also covering her breasts. But, if this is true, it would have been with disregard for Jewish law. Assuming that the attendant is indeed the agent of patriarchal collusion she is implied to be, then we suspect that Goldstein is simply incorrect in assuming that the attendant wants her to cover her breasts while saying the blessing. It is more likely that the attendant would want her to follow Jewish law according to its authentic prescription, which means placing her arms across her midriff, under her heart, and looking out of the water as she says the blessing.[25] Some sources explain that this movement is intended to separate the upper and lower parts of her body, creating a recognition of the higher and lower spiritual forces within a person as well as a recognition that the higher, the holier, should predominate. This separation is required of Jewish males as well during prayer and is accomplished by the wearing of a belt. According to the practical

Ashkenazi *Halakha* of immersion, there is no mention of hiding breasts, and this is not practiced either. Goldstein's inclusion of this inventive aberration alludes to feminism's denunciation of chauvinistic aversions to the female body as shown by menstrual taboos and other superstitions. In one false, flippant phrase, Goldstein throws the mud of this ideological condemnation onto traditional Judaism. Her subversion makes just enough space for the unsubstantiated association of traditional Judaism with superstitious, misogynistic systems. The subversion is housed in the assumption that the ultra–Orthodox *mikvah* attendant would have liked her to cover her breasts while saying the blessing. But the subversion is subtle: The resistance to a contrived expectation of the placement of arms about four inches higher than where they should be allows for a contrived ideological attack. And all this while she dips in a *mikvah* and recites the traditional blessing: important women's rituals as defined by rabbinic (male) renditions of the law. Goldstein's article is an extreme example of Jewish feminism's simultaneous affirmation/condemnation of traditional Judaism, even when focusing on women-centered rituals. Jewish feminist writings such as Goldstein's fostered an across-the-board condemnation of all strains of Jewish feminism by ultra–Orthodox Jews. Goldstein acknowledges ultra–Orthodoxy's disapproval in the figure of the ultra–Orthodox *mikvah* attendant, who "grew weary of what she thought were antics."[26]

More recently, we see that while there is a movement among Jewish women toward the reassessment of traditional Jewish values, there is a parallel, but inverted, movement in a more radical direction. Judith Plaskow's *Standing Again at Sinai* demonstrates this radicalism. She advocates modifications in Jewish theology that reflect the latest feminist theological dialectics. Her discussion focuses on reexaminations of Jewish ritual, liturgy, sexuality, chosenness and divine imaging. She defines her vision of Judaism's "radical transformation" as a "transition" from historical Jewish theology, not a "break." Her commitment to Jewish identity is earnest and apparent. However, her concept of that identity is based on what she determines to be a more female-oriented way of working in the world, namely "fluidity." Thus, she feels no compunctions about working outside of and against *Halakha*. On the contrary, it is the core of Jewish tradition that must be transformed. She acknowledges that Jewish feminism as she envisions it should uproot an entrenched rabbinic Judaism. In this regard, she suggests that Jewish feminism may situate itself by aligning with the various forms of Judaism that "exist in tension with or outright contradiction to ruling ideologies." Yet, some of the religious orders she lists — alongside which Jewish feminism may take its place — are not really anti-rabbinic and continue to this day. Others have been banned and were either terminated long ago, such as the orders of the Essenes and Sadducees, or flourish in the present, such as the Reform movement. Her list of Jewish break-away groups noticeably fails to mention Christianity.[27]

Plaskow struggles to situate Jewish feminism out of her commitment to Judaism no less than to feminism. Yet, her vision of a reworked Judaism — and the eschewing of concepts and practices it entails — is radical enough that one questions if it is not something else she seeks to create. Something meaningful, valid and spiritual — but something else.

Chasm and Closure

In looking at the reactions to Jewish feminism from the ultra–Orthodox point of view, Michael Kaufman vehemently asserts that there is no loyalty to Judaism whatsoever in the brand of Jewish feminism that corresponds to liberal or equal-opportunity feminism, which he calls "masculofeminism." Kaufman's formulation of masculofeminism corresponds to the more ritual-focused elements in Jewish feminism, which is the majority of Jewish feminism. The subversion or adaptation of male-dominated rituals is the Jewish feminist counterpart to demanding equal opportunity.

Kaufman, speaking for ultra–Orthodoxy as a whole, makes plain his opinion that most mainstream Jewish feminists are motivated by an uncritical acceptance of feminist mores at the expense of Jewish values, especially at the expense of feminine essentialism in Judaism. His tone is caustic.

> Jewish masculofeminism, like its secular "de Beauvoirian" counter-
> part, is fundamentally anti-nature. In objecting to the separate
> spheres of men and women, *the Jewish masculofeminist objects to
> Judaism itself*, to a faith and way of life which are designed to maxi-

mize the gifts of nature — to accommodate the natural, irreducible differences between men and women. She revolts against nature because she is unhappy with her lot as a woman. Unwilling to accept the basic fact of her womanhood — let alone rejoice in her femininity — her ultimate revolt, therefore, is not against the Rabbis and not against halachah, but against God.[28]

Currently, it is hard to envision how the chasm that already exists between ultra–Orthodox women and Jewish feminists could be much wider than it already is, having become institutionalized by its incorporation into Jewish studies across college campuses. Hillel Halkin takes note of this phenomenon in an article in a secular Jewish journal. He comments that the influence of radical feminism in the guise of gender studies has undermined the established foundation of contemporary Jewish scholarship, moving far beyond the perceived "radicalism" of a former generation of Jewish scholars. The guilty party is an insipid postmodern irreverence for the tradition of objectivity, which Halkin quickly traces to the influences of Freud and Marx. What this means for what he terms the "new Jewish scholarship" is that "Jewish history is a text to be read between the lines. Nothing in it is what it seems; everything must be 'demystified'; everything conceals a hidden agenda for the exercise of power and control."[29] Halkin points to several influential volumes of Jewish scholarship that demonstrate the trendy feminist treatment of gender as a culturally situated construction. According to Halkin's review, the problematic feature of critical theory in general appears in these volumes as well, to a lesser or greater degree. A theoretical position is prematurely deemed disproved or deconstructed, and on the basis of what is perceived as its ruins, new theoretical foundations are built. The difficulty is that the deconstruction/reconstruction process is often grounded in theory alone and at some point may begin to spurn reality. The intellectual acrobatics of deconstruction cannot credibly form the basis for a decisive new paradigm of circumstances. At most, postmodern scholarship should be considered to offer a new paradigm among the multiplicity of theoretical positions, each accountable for any digressions from heretofore accepted historical accounts. Halkin states in strong terms the danger in eschewing historical objectivity as a methodology: "Once objective evidentiary truth is discarded as a theoretical possibility, let alone as a practical goal, historical writing slides easily into agitprop."[30] This is the fate of much of Jewish scholarship today, Halkin asserts.

This pulling away from a grounding in reality on the theoretical level, Halkin charges, is also what is happening between the new Jewish academic and the common, historical Jew on the social level. The academic with his rhetorical *pilpul*—which is as close to postmodern feminist theory as it is distant from contemporary and ancestral Jewish learning—seems to have lost touch with the collective historical experience of what it means to live as a Jew: to work and struggle amidst adversity alongside a spouse, to feed one's children, to "suffer, fall ill, die, see others die." Halkin responds to the changing face of Jewish scholarship—and most notably to one of its outstanding proponents, Daniel Boyarin—with "something like dread." He sees danger in what such dialectics might mean for an American Jewish identity that is already incohesive and tottering.[31]

Linda Grant, writing in a secular British Jewish magazine, reiterates Halkin's opinion that postmodernist scholars have lost touch with reality. Her article is more tongue-in-cheek than Halkin's, but her basic critique is serious enough. She levels her grievances at gender politics more than gender studies, and with indignation she denounces the sentiment that equity-based liberal feminism is

> obsolete thinking, obsolete feminism that set up power oppositions between the sexes and which had been replaced by "gender studies" which challenged the very notions of biology. For as we all knew, having read Foucault and Lacan, gender was not a biological but a social construction. Rather than being born with our sexual identities, we construct them, they are formed in the world. We are all cross-dressers.[32]

Grant makes the connection between Judaism, feminism and gender studies by making the startling claim that the Jewish "contribution to gender politics is, of course, American second-wave feminism." This surprising statement is based on the thinking that Jewish women, duly following in the path of their faith's rabbinic tradition of legal debate, but unable to exert their "power" within traditional Judaism, took to exerting their power in the world, in the workplace, in the form of gender politics. Her proof is that the leaders of American second-wave feminism were Jewish. She names Betty Friedan,

Gloria Steinem, Barbara Seaman, Andrea Dworkin and Naomi Wolf. The claim of feminism as being a Jewish "contribution" is stated too glibly to be taken seriously, but it is an interesting, almost paradoxical claim. She implies that Jewish women are too strong and that they focused that strength (historically) in business and (contemporarily) in feminist politics. At the same time, she makes the assertion that they "are allowed to play virtually no part in the religious life of their faith."[33] Of course, this is based on her facile summing-up of Judaism as a synagogue-based religion. She is no friend of ultra–Orthodoxy, but she attempts to situate her observation that Jewish women attempted "feminizing" the workplace, i.e., demanding equal opportunity, in place of "feminizing" their own religion. The implicit irony in her argument is that it is based on the Jewish woman not as victim but as natural leader and revolutionary.

Michelene Wandor, another British feminist, also has her problems with feminist theory. In thinking that is reminiscent of Grant, Wandor asserts that maybe the paralysis in Jewish feminism today is that the feminist prototype of woman-as-victim may not be applicable to Jews, that maybe Jewish feminists are wrongly applying the power play inherent in feminist gender paradigms, or that Jewish women should not be looked at as oppressed and powerless but more correctly as the figures of strength they have historically been. Wandor claims that the prototype (or stereotype) of the Jewish mother is overbearing enough, and that instead of looking at where she needs to take control, we should look at where she is vulnerable and should be taken care of. "If we all see ourselves as only rugged independent individuals without any sense of the importance of interdependence, we are — paradoxically — still rooted in a gender divide that remains more destructive than constructive."[34] Wandor ends her article with a bid for interdependence, a gesture that effectively sweeps aside the most complex questions about gender. With everything that was, is and has been, men and women need each other after all, or they should. This single idea seems to be a reversal of the whole theoretical nucleus of feminism as an attempt to establish an identity for women as a separate gender group. Either Wandor's vision represents a new level of radicalism in feminism or, more likely, it expresses a disappointment with where feminism has brought society so far. Wandor's inability to clarify a "right" Jewish women's identity, similar to

Linda Grant's inability to clarify it, is an admission of deep dissatisfaction.

While Grant bitingly blames postmodernist feminist politics and thought for the obfuscation of masculine, feminine and Jewish identities, she, ironically, recognizes the embracing of traditional Judaism as a response that is as valid as any, showing "what a real mess current gender politics are in." She grants a certain tongue-in-cheek validity to women who have "walked voluntarily towards fundamentalism," grateful to escape the clutches of a grasping world.[35] Grant is far from acknowledging traditional Judaism as the "right" response to a faltering feminism, but in the context of a postmodernist consciousness she sarcastically questions who today is capable of claiming ideological dominance: Who can say what you should be doing with your Jewishness or with your consciousness in general? Hers is the voice of feminist disillusionment, if not total despair. Yet, even in despairing feminism, Grant goes down with humor:

> You can dress in leather and get a swastika tattooed on your left
> breast in a misguided attempt to "reclaim" this ancient symbol
> from its current sinister meaning. ... Or you can sit in shul
> [synagogue] under your *shetl* [wig], allied against pornography with
> Andrea Dworkin. Is this mess feminism's failure or its success, its
> capacity to endure, to reshape itself for each new generation? Men
> and women — try doing without them. That's what the animal
> rights protesters dream of, a world without humanity, just trusting,
> caring baby seals and baby calves and, more unfortunately, baby
> mosquitoes. Animal rights is the new movement, the one that makes
> gender seem irrelevant.[36]

In the end, the only common ground between ultra–Orthodox Judaism and Jewish feminism (other than their joint stance against pornography) may be the sort of disillusionment that Grant expresses. The disenchantment with a women's movement that did not achieve its goals, or whose achievements turned in upon itself, leaves an opening for the reconsideration of validating other women's nonfeminist choices (even though the act of making choices is essentially a feminist one). Some ultra–Orthodox proponents suggest other points of reconciliation with feminism, which we will look at later. Additionally, the gap between traditional Judaism and Jewish feminism may begin to close as the *teshuva* movement, the movement of secular Jews taking on traditional Jewish practice, keeps its momentum. Sincere feminists who become ultra–Orthodox bring with them a sensitivity and awareness of feminist issues — and a potential for closing the gap between ultra–Orthodox Jewish women and mainstream Jewish feminists. In the writings of these *baalot teshuva* (newly Orthodox Jewish women), we can see the outlines of a "feminism" that respects traditional Judaism and the woman's role in it, while it insists on grappling with the issues feminism has raised. It is plausible to envision how this ultra–Orthodox "feminism" would be for Jewish feminism what essentialist feminism is for mainstream feminism, i.e., a more organic, difference-focused, if not mystic understanding of the feminine.

The gap between ultra–Orthodox and feminist Jewish women may also begin to close as certain streams of the larger feminist movement move toward revaluing traditional female roles, such as motherhood. Jewish women who are disappointed with the array of feminist ideologies, or jaded feminists who are disillusioned by what the sexual revolution has meant in their lives, approach issues of marriage and motherhood with a sensitivity born of hard experience.

Writer Elizabeth Powers claims in an article in a secular Jewish journal that women's liberation has begotten a generation of women who cannot enjoy the fruits of their labor: The slighting, or even forfeiture, of their feminine potentials as wife and mother has embittered any career gains that the women's movement made possible. Powers also blames early liberal feminism, and especially the sexual revolution it engendered, for fostering a generation of men who have been released from accountability to women as husbands and fathers. The result, Powers asserts, is that while the women's movement promised to free women from the societal entrapment of sexual objectification, women are as objectified today as ever.[37]

In the search to regain the prestige and power of the mother and her home, Jewish feminists like Powers may revalue religious Jewish women's literature for its veneration of the family structure with the Jewish mother at its core. Ultra-Orthodox women's literature demonstrates that, far from being peripheral in Jewish life, women are central. However, this centrality takes a different form, questioning the whole preoccupation with an exclusivist centrality, which has been the mainstay of feminist thought. Current feminist and cultural theories are moving away from preestablished assumptions of women's sameness, oppression and marginality. Centrality as a woman — even in interrelational roles as mother and wife — is a concept whose ramifications mainstream feminism has yet to explore in earnest, a concept that ultra–Orthodox Jewish women's literature may infuse into places where feminist consciousness flounders.

Another site of amalgamation between ultra–Orthodoxy and Jewish feminism is Orthodox feminism and the academic proponents associated with that movement. Orthodox feminism is a movement of modern Orthodox or traditional Jews who embrace feminism. The level of observance of Orthodox feminists varies greatly, but they do not usually approach the stringency of ultra–Orthodox observance. Orthodox feminist critics have often been ideologically aligned with feminism more than with Orthodoxy. Their treatment of Jewish sources has often displayed an irreverence for traditional understandings of Torah and *Halakha* (the entire body of legal rulings in traditional Judaism) and an insensitivity toward the traditionalists' veneration of the rabbinic interpreters of law. They were deemed by ultra–Orthodox Jews as forcing a view of traditional Judaism through the critical prism of feminism, making the feminist agenda the standard of judgment. However, this is not necessarily true today, when many Jewish women of varying levels of observance have achieved literacy in Jewish legal sources. In examining those sources, the feminist, traditionalist academics have found a greater endorsement for women in Judaism. Thus, from within biblical and rabbinic sources, some Orthodox feminists have acknowledged that traditional Judaism can accommodate more feminist visions of religious participation than was previously thought.[38]

Reactionary Infrastructure in Critical Theory

Having examined an array of Jewish feminist writings, we can better understand the reactionary infrastructure of ultra–Orthodox women's literature, an infrastructure based both on the charges the literature was responding to and on the sociopolitical context in which its writers began and continue their work. We can also understand the reactionary basis in a noncontextual sense, that is, from the point of view of literary critical theory. We can look especially at textual criticisms in general in their connection to reader-response criticism. Locating the reactionary infrastructure, in turn, helps to explain why the literature is relatively so late in blooming: It gathered momentum in reaction to Jewish feminism. It waited for the provocation of another movement, as it were.

Nelly Furman in "Textual Feminism" points out that "for the feminist scholar, the importance of textual criticism resides in the implications of the switch to the power of the reader. ... Reading is no longer just an attempt to decipher; it is simultaneously a gesture of self-inscription."[39] This helps us understand that every reading is indeed a new literary form, a criticism in itself; that literature by nature is reactionary. "Furthermore, the reader is not a passive consumer, but an active producer of a new text. The reader's text is the medium which can give voice and visibility to a feminist literary consciousness."[40]

Ferdinand de Saussure envisioned language as a system of signifiers and the signified, or words and their meanings. Both are arbitrary and fluctuating.[41] The implication of de Saussure's system, which later critics such as Roland Barthes developed, is that any text can generate many meanings, as many as there are readers. Every reader constructs her own meaning, which, in turn, becomes a criticism of the original meaning (and a criticism of the value of criticism itself). The generation of a new text means the generation of new meanings, and critical discourse, ultimately, has no closure.

The positive product of this cycle is the constant generation of new meanings, new texts. Supported by literary criticism, we can erect the premise of the reactionary nature of literature in general and ultra–Orthodox women's literature in particular. This gives conceptual depth to the assertion that the response of ultra–Orthodox women to Jewish feminist literature actually resulted in a new genre. The resistance to ideas perceived as foreign and threatening — to writing that could not faithfully represent all Jewish female readers — spurred the creation of a new body of writing that did speak for those readers. Ultra-Orthodox women's literature, therefore, is a (not necessarily conscious) reaction to and criticism of Jewish feminism. As a literary response to literature, it is a spontaneous, credible portrayal of the community that writes and reads it.

CHAPTER TWO

Ultra-Orthodox Women's Voices as "Other"

In exploring the cultural atmosphere in which religious women's writing takes place, it is important to discuss two academic books that have been influential and widely read, even among ultra–Orthodox women. This promotes an understanding of the popular assertion that ultra–Orthodox writing innately resists the conceptual milieu in and against which it works. Both books are written by non–Orthodox Jewish women, and both treat ultra–Orthodox women's voices as "other." The first is Debra Renee Kaufman's *Rachel's Daughters: Newly Orthodox Jewish Women*.

Kaufman's book is a sociological study of *baalot teshuva*, which is the Hebrew term for Jewish women who were raised secular but have taken on religious practice as adults. She interviews and observes 150 newly Orthodox and ultra–Orthodox women. Her study is unique in that it is an attempt to evaluate the lives of religious women from within the Orthodox world. It is an attempt to bridge cultural discrepancies, to solve the problem of Schweickart's ellipsis.

The novelty of Kaufman's study is that she gives the Orthodox women a real voice — their own voice — by presenting large chunks of the women's words verbatim. In simply presenting religious Jewish women as they see themselves, her study is beneficial and innovative. By listening to those voices, certain presuppositions are exposed that will help us understand the mentality of the religious Jewish woman writer.

It seems to me that the most important aspect of the ultra–Orthodox literature is the feeling expressed by Kaufman's interviewees of being part of the larger community without feeling inferior as women:

The ba'alot teshuvah share the "official" patriarchal belief system of Orthodox Judaism and a belief system that emerges organically from their everyday lives as women in a highly sex-segregated community. They believe that community is critical if Orthodox Jewish life is to be preserved. For them, female activities and systems of meaning are as vital to Orthodox Judaism as are men's. They do not see their sphere as inferior, but rather as a place where ... they are free to create their own forms of personal, social, intellectual, and, at times, political relationships....

They seem to expand the domestic limits set by patriarchal living, not by entering a man's world, but by creating a world of their own. The solidarity, self-esteem, and strength they receive from this world reinforces them in their celebration of difference and woman-centered values and in making claims upon the community as a whole for care, commitment, and connectedness.[42]

Kaufman's study helps us understand religious Jewish women's literature in two ways: by showing us the sense of empowerment that the women express, which we will later see in their literature, and, ironically, by showing us how Jewish feminists like herself repress that expression.

Kaufman's book is a veritable paradox. Kaufman is unable to grant validity to the voices that she herself presents. Her attempt to understand the cultural "otherness" of ultra–Orthodox women fails. In her preface, she admits the otherness of Jewish Orthodoxy to her: "Why had these women seemingly turned away from any number of the Western liberation movements ... to religion? Why would youth exposed to alternative life-styles consciously choose such a traditional context as adults? As an 'orthodox' feminist, I could not understand such a political 'cop-out.'"[43]

She sees the paradox of these newly Orthodox and ultra–Orthodox women's choice and sets out to understand it, but in the end she makes little progress from where she began. Her fear of nonscientificism is obstructive:

Many readers may believe I have given too much credence to the women's own words ... that I am unable to see them objectively or analytically. Therefore, it is now time for me to take up their narratives from the standpoint of a feminist social scientist ... to place these narratives in an ongoing dialectic between history and the present and between institutions and the individual.[44]

She hardly succeeds in achieving those goals, which was exactly what was necessary. She brought us the women's voices, but what she does not bring us, among other insights, is the larger cultural background of traditional Judaism's "ongoing dialectic between history and the present." We must have a *Jewish* perspective, not just a secular sociological one, if we are to appropriate an understanding of these women and their choice to adopt ultra–Orthodox Jewish practice.

If we listen to the narratives of these newly Orthodox and ultra–Orthodox Jewish women, we hear them tell about how they have discovered in traditional Judaism an understanding of the "feminine" which speaks to them on the deepest levels, an appreciation and empowerment as women. This is what we need to understand and research first of all, but Kaufman jumps to a different question, namely whether or not these women are deceiving themselves: "These newly Orthodox Jewish women appear to the reader to have omitted from their stories the 'real' oppressiveness and personal disappointments of religious patriarchy."[45] Kaufman's assumption is too impulsive, uninvestigated and beleaguered with a personal bias that assumes that traditional Judaism could not possibly empower her subjects as women. One hundred and fifty newly Orthodox and ultra–Orthodox Jewish women reinforce one another's assertion of feminine endorsement in traditional Judaism. The assumption of across-the-board self-deception seems farfetched but not impossible —*if* it can be proved, or nearly proved, or at least made plausible. But, since Kaufman does not attempt such an undertaking, the most radical issue her research raises is not the assumption of self-deception, but the question of what if they are not deceiving themselves? What do the women's convictions mean if taken at face value? This is a vital question that must be answered before we can conclude that there is irrationality or self-delusion in their choices. And what are the implications of a set of "patriarchal" laws that are designed in such a way that women feel empowered?

It is clear that Kaufman shies away from the heart of the matter on this and other issues that require an examination of the Jewish laws themselves and a consideration of what aspects of these laws might engender the feeling of empowerment that her interviewees describe. If, after an examination of the laws, she could find no reason for the *baalot teshuva*'s enthusiasm with them, then it would be plausible to consider their enthusiasm self-styled or delusive. This would be more scientifically valid than assuming self-deception in spite of their seeming intelligence and soundness of mind. Kaufman toes a line not uncommon in popular critical inquiry by invalidating the subject of her research too early; by seeking out her opponents' internal contradiction before examining the complexity of their stance; and by insisting that there *must* be contradiction and not just harmonious multiplicity. In Kaufman's case, this translates into a presumption that the women *must* be deceiving themselves because we cannot read oppression in their words.

It is helpful to bear in mind Judith Butler's formulation of mainstream feminism's (and especially difference feminism's) "urgency" to support its political importance as representative of all women by assigning universal status to male domination. This has "occasionally motivated the shortcut to a categorical or fictive universality of the structure of domination, held to produce women's common subjugated experience."[46]

In Kaufman's book, we hear women telling us that they have put themselves within a system that values them, in their most feminine capacities, no less than men, if not more. They tell us of a system that they feel empowers them in their own women-centered domains. I would term what they are describing a matriarchy. If their power, their matriarchy, is no less influential than men's power as patriarchs, then we have a picture of a patriarchy and a matriarchy side by side. A patriarchy that does not dominate the realms that the matriarchy dominates, and is ultimately no more valued than the matriarchy, is defused of the assumption that it is oppressive. So again, could there be an unoppressive patriarchy within traditional Judaism alongside a matriarchy? Or, if the realm of the matriarchy within Judaism is finally overshadowed by that of the patriarchy, then are we looking at a true, unoppressive, if not liberating, patriarchy?[47] And if we do not ask ourselves these questions and instead work with assumptions of the women's self-deception, we are still left with the question of what are these women talking so positively about? Why did they make the choices they did? Kaufman does not analyze these questions even though the narratives of her subjects beg that they be asked.

Kaufman writes:

> Gender identity is key to these newly Orthodox Jewish women. It
> has been crucial to different constituencies in the feminist move-
> ment. Women have used their gender identity culturally to resist or
> challenge aspects of patriarchy, capitalism, technology, and even
> feminism.... Gender identity has been used both for political
> accommodation and resistance.... As of now, these women cannot
> make claims which transcend collective patriarchal interpretation.
> But what of their daughters?[48]

From whichever angle the *baalot teshuva* approached Orthodoxy
and ultra–Orthodoxy, the key to their continued interest is the positive location of their femininity *and* spirituality within an age-old
system. Kaufman's negative predictions for the daughters of *baalot
teshuva* are based on a *non sequitur*, then. Her claim is that the women
ultimately became religious because gender identity is a popular feminist response at this particular time in history. The implication is that
Orthodoxy offered them gender identity within a patriarchal system,
and since gender identity was important to them, they accepted the
system. But, considering that "no patriarchal setting is ever the same
as another in time and location,"[49] the daughters might resist the mothers' response, she concludes.

Again, Jewish reality is not addressed here. We cannot dismiss
traditional Judaism as another fluctuating patriarchy. These women
chose to take on very ancient, largely unchanging laws. This is one
patriarchy that does not fluctuate by and large, so on what grounds
does she insinuate that the daughters' response will be resistance? The
teshuva movement began in the mid–1960s. Scores of daughters of
baalot teshuva have grown since then. Yet, we are still talking about
the ongoing *teshuva* movement without witnessing resistance to that
movement from within it. It seems that even recent history cannot
support Kaufman's skeptical predictions.

In the end, Kaufman demonstrates an incapacity to accept or at
least give credence to the women she interviews. She is unable to grant
and examine the feminine realization of these women as they tell it,
so she undermines the potency of their own narratives and replaces it
with her own regressive scenarios. She is condemned in the end by
her sociological stance as an outsider or, perhaps, by her own Jewish
femininity, which excludes her from ever being truly outside these
particular subjects.

Rachel's Daughters: Newly Orthodox Jewish Women serves the dual purpose of letting us hear how ultra–Orthodox women talk about themselves and letting us see the treatment of their voice by a Jewish feminist. I believe that it is this treatment that is largely responsible for fueling religious women to talk about themselves in their own voice *in their own literature.*

An unpublished manuscript by religious woman writer Chaya Rivkah Jessel, "When Two Worlds Collide: Ultra-Orthodox Women Talk About Their Judaism and Feminism," is evidence that Debra Kaufman's study incited resistance among ultra–Orthodox women. Jessel, a sociologist, actually replicated Kaufman's method of interviewing *baalot teshuva*; however, she was more discerning in the women she chose to interview. She only recorded women who were extremely committed feminists in their secular pasts (some of whom still consider themselves feminists) and who now define themselves as no less than ultra–Orthodox. Jessel's purpose was to record the women's voices that underscore the ideological shift in their move to become religious, voices that pinpoint the conceptual divergence as they discovered and chose to embrace traditional Judaism.

The women discuss the hard-core feminist issues in their becoming religious. They reveal, they confess and, here again, as in Kaufman's work, a universal claim is heard in the women's voices: a claim of feminine empowerment in traditional Judaism. Jessel's aim is largely to redo what Kaufman did, to present the voices of *baalot teshuva* but without Kaufman's analysis, which Jessel rejects as a religious Jewish woman and *baalat teshuva* herself. She seeks to let the women speak for themselves and be granted critical validity: Their words should be taken at face value with an assumption that they mean what they say and do not deceive themselves, consciously or unconsciously. Jessel's work is a manifestation of the sentiment that Kaufman's presentation of the voices of *baalot teshuva* should not be the final word on the subject.

Educated and Ignorant?

Tamar El-Or's book, *Educated and Ignorant: Ultraorthodox Jewish Women and Their World*, is another sociological study about ultra–Orthodox Jewish women.[50] Her study was originally published in Hebrew and is quite different from Kaufman's or Jessel's work. El-Or literally enters the world of a particular group of young Hasidic women in Israel. She makes contact and grows close with one woman who is especially strict in her observance and through her makes other acquaintances. She spends plenty of time with them, observes them, befriends them, talks with them, goes to the places they go and respects their boundaries. In their presence, El-Or covers her hair and dresses modestly, as they do. She never asks them about personal matters, such as their relationships with their husbands, which they clearly do not present as topics for discussion.

El-Or is astute in her observations, although less astute in her analysis. Her observations prove that she has physically made her way "in." She sees what there is to see of the everyday life of ultra–Orthodox (Hasidic) women. However, her analysis shows that she is still an observer from the outside and not really "in." Or, perhaps the real problem is one of cultural appropriation. The picture she presents of ultra–Orthodox life and its paradoxes is surprisingly accurate and non-judgmental. However, when she tries to understand those paradoxes, the tools at her disposal are inadequate. Her lack of acquired Jewish knowledge, along with her secular, academic approach, make the accuracy of her conclusions fall short of the quality of her observations.

The main theme that runs throughout her book is represented by her interpretation of the quote below, which she presents in an epithet. She quotes the late Rabbi Avraham Yosef Wolf, who was the founder and principal of the Beit Ya'akov College for Girls in Bene Brak, an ultra–Orthodox institution in Israel: "If we succeed in instilling in our girl students that the purpose of their studies is to aspire to emulate our matriarchs, who did not study, then we have succeeded in educating our daughters."[51] El-Or presents her understanding of the paradox of ultra–Orthodox women's education thus: They are educated to be ignorant. Her understanding is theoretically possible, even probable, yet it is inaccurate because she does not ground it in the findings indicated by her observations or in a Jewish context.

She observes that the ultra–Orthodox women — who spend much of their day caring for their young children at home — use most of their spare time in learning sessions. Many of them work as teachers, and most are graduates of institutions of higher Jewish education. They attend regular classes and study sessions, usually led by other women.

These are vibrant sessions for the most part, displaying the women's personal stake in understanding the subject matter. El-Or observes the importance that education, specifically voluntary Jewish education, has in these women's lives, even after their formal education ended and they are burdened with the demands of children and home.

She also observes that the women prefer and relate to practical subject matter, such as Jewish law, which pertains to their everyday lives. She asserts that they are adverse to, if not incapable of, abstract thinking. They are preoccupied with justifying their study, with which subjects they should and should not study, with what is relevant and permissible for them to study, with the purpose of their study. They feel the need to constantly ground their study with a tangible, useful purpose and message. They do not rely on their own interpretive abilities and refer these powers to their authoritative teachers. They only feel comfortable with passing on information, not generating it. And insofar as these attitudes toward education, or noneducation, were instilled in them by the very people and institutions that educate them; they are educated to be ignorant, her argument goes, a virtual paradox. El-Or is astute in sensing that a paradox exists where women's education is concerned, but the crux of her analysis of that paradox would be very different had she based it on her own observations and augmented it with a knowledge of Jewish law.

El-Or opens her book with a detailed description of Hannah and some of the neighbors and acquaintances in Hannah's life. Hannah is more strictly observant than most of the ultra–Orthodox women in her environment and is recognized as such, we are told. This gains Hannah respect, but she also experiences others' envy and isolation. El-Or tells us that discerning Hannah's exceptionality actually enabled her to discern the social norm among ultra–Orthodox women more easily.

The observations she makes about Hannah and her neighbors are put forth without much critical evaluation. This uncritical stance is a pleasant surprise rather than a fault. It saves El-Or from passing judgment on the women she describes, which would be retrogressive rather than helpful: Faulty judgments can be passed just by dint of being a human being in close social situations with very different human beings. However, there is a basic evaluation, a necessary analysis, that El-Or does not contend with: What is it about Hannah that makes her recognized as more observant and therefore deserving of respect? It is important to understand which factors put a person on a higher or lower status in her particular society, as this dynamic affects the whole social edifice. Understanding the parameters of value judgments in the ultra–Orthodox world helps us understand how ultra–Orthodox Jews make the decisions they make; what their underlying motivations are. El-Or carefully presents the raw material that can reveal the social impetus driving ultra–Orthodox Jewish women. Yet, she does not aim to explain the social dynamic in their world based on that material. This is a necessary ingredient in her and our understanding of ultra–Orthodox women's education. In identifying basic motivational forces in ultra–Orthodox women's lives, we will understand other aspects of their lives, such as education. To pinpoint the ultra–Orthodox women's social motive, we should seek to ask, What do they see as being socially superior, as making one a better woman? What do they strive toward, what theme circumscribes their lives, and why?

We can turn to El-Or's own observations for the answers. The easiest place to start is the most obvious place: Hannah. Hannah is the focus of her neighbors' curiosity, but most of all she is the focus of their respect. This is because she is recognized as being more strictly observant. We need only examine a few of the most visible and obvious differences between Hannah and her neighbors in order to understand what underlying principles unite those differences. The most apparent difference between Hannah and most of the other women is that Hannah covers her hair with a scarf, not a wig. Assuming that modesty is the main reason behind the ultra–Orthodox women's hair covering,[52] we see that Hannah has chosen to be more modest than the norm. That is, if the point of the hair covering is modesty, then Hannah focuses on that point and carries it to an extreme. El-Or tells us that there are many gradations of wigs and their greater or lesser level of modesty. All the women follow the conventions of Jewish modesty; however, unlike Hannah, their own desire to look beautiful shares a part in their routines of adornment. They do not go against the customs of modesty that their environment defines, but rather they temper the application of that modesty with their own instinctive will, a will that inherently stands in opposition to the thrust of modesty. From El-Or's descriptions we see that more modest women follow the dictates of their personal will to a lesser degree, and vice versa. Women who follow Jewish dictates more closely, even as it opposes their own inclination to adorn themselves, were considered to be more modest, thus more stringent and also more admirable.

Hannah chose to implement modesty to an extreme degree, which was consistent with her strict implementation of all the Jewish precepts. She did this by adopting Judaism's will as her own will, by abnegating her natural desires and focusing on the ideological intention of the Jewish precept. Even on a minimalistic level, Jewish observancy requires a move of accommodation where the tradition runs counter to personal preferences. On a maximalistic level, observancy requires something more than self-abnegation. It requires a re-making of the self. One focuses on the spirit of the law, not only the letter of the law. One focuses on the goal of the tradition and working toward the goal, even where the minimal requirements for practice have already been met. Thus, if Hannah is required to cover her hair according to Jewish tradition, and if the point, the goal, of that precept is modesty, then Hannah aims unyieldingly at modesty in hair covering, not just a minimalistic level of hair covering.

We see throughout El-Or's description of the ultra–Orthodox world a focus on the intent of Jewish law and a shunning of anything superfluous to that intent. This outlook shapes the women's motivation to act in every respect. Hannah's house, for example, contains none of the superfluous decorative items found in the other women's homes. What El-Or describes to us is a society that is extremely goal-oriented. Thus, stricter observancy can be seen in the emphasis that one places on realizing the goal or intent of Jewish law, a refining of practice beyond the minimalistic observance by which one fulfills her requirements. Even where one can claim exemption from the law for valid reasons, a maximalistic, or goal, orientation ensures that exemptions are usually employed only when necessary.[53]

We see the extreme way Hannah controls her children's education, examining every toy and book at night while the children sleep before allowing it to pass into their hands the next day. Another example of this principle is Hannah's husband who learns Torah full time, as do most of the women's husbands. But he does so by leaving home for most of the week, which ensures that he is totally absorbed in his study. Hannah concurs with his devotion to study. If the intent of the *mitzvah* is continual, concentrated study, then he focuses on that intent. We see their maximalistic, goal-oriented application to Jewish tradition.

According to ultra–Orthodox sensibilities, inasmuch as Jewish laws are deemed to be ultimately granted by an ever-engaged, ever-attentive divinity, the importance of their implementation is as important as life itself. No scrutiny of what is the goal of a Jewish precept and how best to achieve it is trivial. No legal analyses lie outside the realm of relevancy when they can lead to an understanding of why, but mostly how, to act. Thus, the whole point of a goal-oriented outlook in the ultra–Orthodox world is the fulfillment of the holy will. This scrutiny of Jewish commandments is considered holy in and of itself because it too is one of the holy precepts. Learning Torah can be understood in part as the most important *mitzvah*, or divinely commanded act, because it circumscribes all other acts.

Learning Torah in the Jewish world cannot be compared to literacy in the academic sense, because it is not celebrated only as an intellectual activity. It takes a primary place among the acts derived from the Torah that are incumbent upon Jews according to Jewish tradition. Inasmuch as the continual expounding of the Torah is a directive, an act, then a Jew is exempt from Torah learning only if another act supersedes it in importance at that moment, such as an act that cannot be pushed off or performed by someone else. The importance of performing the most important of acts (studying Torah) is superseded only by the performance of another imperative act. In the ultra–Orthodox world, the determining factor in choosing a course of action is based on a question of priorities, of which act is more important at a particular time. What we need to derive from the example of Torah study is the extreme importance of prioritizing as a prerequisite for goal-oriented action in the ultra–Orthodox world.

The ultra–Orthodox women El-Or observes — who leave their small children and household obligations to study Torah — are constantly compelled to reformulate the goals of their Torah study. El-Or observes that the women feel relieved to ground their study in the legalities of practical observance. She hears that they feel a need to justify their study. And she concludes that this justification represents the women's complicity in the cultural imperative to keep women ignorant. But, based on the extreme goal orientation in ultra–Orthodox society — on the constant filtering of ideas and behavior for ideological purity — we can draw a cross-reference to the women's educational practices.

A religious and cultural imperative in the ultra–Orthodox world stresses learning Torah; another imperative stresses the importance of raising and educating children, of Jewish life in the home sphere. The mother is the center of this sphere, and it is here that her primary obligations lie. Guarding the home-centered aspects of Judaism, including mothering, is her primary holy act in Jewish perception. To leave small children, to leave the home at a stage in life when the obligations generated by the home are pressing, is to throw into doubt the validity of her excusing herself from her primary act (mothering) in order to perform an act that is secondary for her (studying Torah).[54]

The dilemma is especially acute in the case of these young women because the divinely prescribed act, which is secondary for them, is none other than that which is primary in general. This leads to a certain pressure not to waste spare time but to spend it in Torah study, which El-Or notices. This is further complicated by the historical exemption of women from Torah study, especially certain areas of study. This exemption serves to stress the primacy of their roles as mothers and homemakers, roles that are particularly demanding for most of them. Women's historical exclusion from certain areas of Torah study also creates a backdrop of pressure not to enter those intellectual domains. And all this, even as women's exemption from Torah study today is understood differently, even as Torah study has effectively been made obligatory for them as they grew up, and even as they are still obligated to perform the acts (Torah commandments) which that study circumscribes.[55] As a result, the women feel relieved to study Torah that is concrete and applicable in their immediate lives, to take some lesson home with them. This serves to justify their choice of prioritizing study over the home at that moment. It also demonstrates how ultra–Orthodox women infuse the question of choice into their actions, how they are faced with a continual reevaluation of their process of choosing.

Thus, as mentioned, a paradoxical situation arises where Torah study is a means for understanding how to act according to the Torah's commandments, and a goal in itself because it *is* a Torah commandment. The act is framed in the study, and the study is framed in the act. The historical exemption of women from the act of studying Torah as a goal (but not as a means) can partly be understood by the intention of any exemption: to enable the fulfillment of a *mitzvah* that takes precedence at that time, such as caring for the needs of one's children. If we apply the goal orientation that El-Or observes in ultra–Orthodox society, and posit her observations in a traditional Jewish context, we can conclude that the paradox of women's learning that Rabbi Wolf referred to is not that women should study in order to understand that they should not study, but that they should study in order to understand that the deed, the action, in Judaism is always primary. Or, in his own negative phraseology: *not* to study Torah as a goal in itself but as a means to the goal of keeping the Torah.

El-Or records her impression that the ultra–Orthodox women she studied are not inclined to abstract thinking and that their "education for ignorance" may in fact have made them incapable of it. It is clear that the women do not prefer abstract thinking in general. But the most specific example she gives of their inability to work within abstractions is actually an exception, a clear example of their ability to emulate the classical Jewish learning mode of deconstructing and reconstructing knowledge categories.

She records a debate in a study session in which the women argued over the terms used to categorize the constituents of a permissible way to do a forbidden act on the Sabbath. If this description sounds confusing, it is because it is indeed abstract. The women's goal was to learn how to stay clear of forbidden activities on the Sabbath. They did not just learn what was forbidden but under what conditions it became permissible. In doing so, they entered into the classical mode of naming/constructing categories and then (re)defining objects within those categories. And they went beyond a reiteration of the basic permitted action and grasped the hermeneutics behind the *Halakha*. By naming categories and defining which objects are included in those categories, a permissible way of doing the forbidden act is established. They argued about the names of the categories, about how those names ineffectively define the categories. They argued that the names that define the categories effectively raise more questions than they answer. The women's debate as El-Or records it seems almost comical *because* it is so abstract. But it is no more comical than the hair-splitting halakhic debates in the Talmud, which are reiterated again and again in male institutions of Jewish scholarship.

It seems to El-Or that the women cannot make the jump from the practical to the abstract because their intention was to simply review the laws of the Sabbath, a practical, educational goal. In the course of that review, the women argued over the terms of the categorization on which the *Halakha* is based. They got stuck in debate over the problematics of the halakhic terminology. They got stuck in the abstract, while to El-Or and (not ironically) to the one woman in the group who came from a secular background, it seemed that the women couldn't grasp the abstract.

The crux of the misinterpretation has to do with the distance of El-Or and the *baalat teshuva* from classical modes of Jewish learning and the assimilation of these modes by the ultra–Orthodox women. This learning is predicated on the understanding that not only do humans construct knowledge, but that by constructing knowledge we are constructing reality: To name is to define. By defining the world, we are constructing the world. Thus deconstructing a theoretical category in the edifice of knowledge has a direct bearing on how one acts. Arguing about how we name the idea of something is arguing about how one should act based on that knowledge. We construct our knowledge categories — and therefore effectively construct our realities, our actions and our lives. But in posing the ever-present question of whether what one does is right, all knowledge constructions must be grounded in and limited by the holy will as a transcendent truth system. Judaism deconstructs the dichotomous tension between the abstract and the concrete, between the theoretical and the practical. They become different shades of the same unified reality, which is informed by Torah/truth, a reality that then informs human constructions of knowledge and action.

To El-Or, the Hasidic women seemed to approach a theoretical argument from a practical standpoint, an indication that they may lack the ability to think abstractly. She adds this understanding to bolster her thesis of the women's education for ignorance. Her own academic background distinguishes between the practical and the abstract, and one need not have any bearing on the other. But, when the final analysis of the abstract answers the question of how one lives one's life, then the abstract and the practical encompass and inform one another. This difference in mindset between El-Or and the women she studies is stated in an article written after the publication of *Educated and Ignorant*.

El-Or describes the reaction of other ultra–Orthodox women to her description of the women's debate in the study session:

> The reading group I had set up to critique my thesis — four ultra-orthodox women from the Gur sect, but not from the community I studied — also smiled at this section. Miriam, a senior teacher at Beit Yaakov, said: "Well, this is funny. Sure, I can see why people laugh, it could sound stupid. I'm not saying it didn't happen or that you're describing it incorrectly, but I'm sure we're laughing for different reasons. You're wondering whether they couldn't get it, but I know they did. I smile because I hear something familiar, understood, like meeting an old girlfriend. I smile because I know what was actually going on in their minds and hearts. You see it from your academic standpoint, I see it from our lives."[56]

In this later article, based on the reactions to her book, El-Or seems to have reconsidered her conclusions about the women's debate in the study session. Here she admits that the women's "discussion that ensued in that example presents the halakhic way of thinking as a manipulation, as a juggling of 'truths.'"[57] Here again, her analysis is not wrong *per se*, but it's not right either. Her heightened understanding is that ultra–Orthodox women, who lack the "social legitimacy and intellectual preparation" to deconstruct and reread male-defined frameworks, "work, instead, with a subtle resistance."[58] She plugs these women's studies into the power paradigm of gender studies. El-Or's implication is that the resistant reading of the women in the study group follows (albeit far behind) the deconstruction and rereading process of feminists, that when ultra–Orthodox Jewish women read critically, they resist "male-defined constructs" as part of the movement to "negotiate men's literacy." Such an assertion misses the mark. When ultra–Orthodox women's learning displays a critical or resistant tone, it cannot be comfortably explained by an analogy to feminist literary resistance. It rather begs an analogy to the male Jewish learning that surrounds the women through the men and boys in their lives.

The whole thrust of Jewish knowledge constructions is based on resistance. This is what fills the Talmud. Men reading these texts read with resistance in order to enter into the deconstruction/reconstruction process, which is how the knowledge of the Talmud is acquired.

This is not to say that men's resistant reading constructs or generates knowledge, but that it invests itself in constructed knowledge. Resistant reading is engaged reading, and it is certainly the way a resistant text such as the Talmud begs to be learned. Compendiums of halakhic rulings and other philosophical and ethical works of Jewish scholarship, which are the type of texts women are inclined to study, do not necessarily have to be studied with resistance. But, here too, engaged reading is resistant reading. It is therefore more plausible to assume that when ultra–Orthodox women read critically, they are reproducing the type of resistant learning style that pervades their environment through their fathers, husbands, sons and teachers. In other words, they are learning like Jewish men. Insofar as insulated, Hasidic women who were raised in religious homes are as far from feminism as they are close to Jewish men's learning, El-Or's association of them with feminist "protest," as she calls it, is arbitrary and inaccurate. It reflects an attempt to fit the "square" of feminist paradigms into the "circle" of traditional Judaism. Ironically, this seems to be El-Or's way of redeeming the subjects of her research: by conferring an ill-suited feminist progressiveness — a sort of forced heroism — upon them.

CHAPTER THREE

Self-affirmation as Response

The literature of ultra–Orthodox Jewish women is a reaction to secular Jewish feminism, as already stated. But what type of reaction? When we look at the literature, we see that feminism is usually addressed indirectly. The amount of literature that deals directly with feminist issues is relatively small but quickly growing. Even there, a direct response to feminism might only be found in the book's preface or introduction. This response is not even meant for feminists' ears but for those of religious Jewish women. The more common response to feminism, however, that which we find between the lines of most texts, is indirect — an inward reflection and self-strengthening. We see the ultra–Orthodox community reflecting upon and reaffirming the roles that women have traditionally played in its culture.[59] This reflection and reaffirmation can range from erudite analysis to impassioned polemics.

The response of self-affirmation is not exclusively a women's response, rather it is one that has been used by both ultra–Orthodox men and women, albeit in different ways. It is as if, being attacked from the outside, the ultra–Orthodox community chooses to reaffirm its communal female identity instead of responding to the source of the attack. This shows that the ultra–Orthodox community is concerned with protecting the female half of its identity more than rhetorically blasting its detractors, to protect what it already has and not to create what it does not by forging an identity through differentiation and detraction. It also shows that the ultra–Orthodox community as a whole perceives that it embraces a viable, female identity to protect. Since the ultra–Orthodox community's response to feminism can be said to be reluctant, the actuality of a response shows the extent of the inroads made by feminism into ultra–Orthodox circles.

It is plausible to generalize that self-affirming literature appears in two forms: critical/scholarly and prosaic/creative. Generally, critical works that reaffirm the traditional position of the Jewish woman have mostly been written by men, while women's defense or reaffirming of their own positions has usually been expressed in their creative prose. So again, ultra–Orthodox women's literature is ideologically an extension of the attempt to grapple with the encroachment of Jewish feminist consciousness. Since we will closely examine the women's prose later, we will now briefly focus on different aspects of ultra–Orthodox critical literature that discusses women in Judaism.

Perhaps the earliest response to feminism is Moshe Meiselman's *Jewish Woman in Jewish Law*. Meiselman makes plain his intention to present an authentic evaluation of Jewish law concerning issues on which feminism focused. Thus, his early "rejoinder" was not so much an engagement of issues as an attempt to set Judaism's record straight, to enable constructive dialogue by clarifying issues that had been distorted and confused. The overall tone of Meiselman's study is respectful of feminism as far as feminist assertions agree with Jewish ideals. But it is also blunt in its criticism where feminist theory contradicts or falls short of the Jewish outlook. Feminist arguments are not addressed in detail, but they are clearly the context against which his discussion becomes relevant. The exception to this is his ideological rejoinder to Rachel Adler's "The Jew Who Wasn't There: *Halakha* and the Jewish Woman."[60] His response is unique in that the majority of works by traditional critics do not respond to or mention specific feminist works.

Another example of this inward-focused literature reaffirming the woman's position, particularly as mother, is Yisroel Miller's *In Search of the Jewish Woman: A Torah Journey*. This work is typical of the indirect ultra–Orthodox response to feminism. The bid to justify the traditional woman's role is clear. That it only addresses the religious Jewish community is also clear. There is no direct confrontation with feminist issues, but there *is* a rousing call for religious women to appreciate their culture amidst the perceived degradation by feminism.

Miller means to open a discussion of the philosophical approach of traditional Judaism to the position of women. He feels that modern culture confuses the traditional role of women, making it seem inferior and unclear. Women have lost their sense of purpose. Miller wants to go beyond the halakhic discussions of women, beyond the "how" of the Jewish woman's role to the "why."

Miller argues that the traditional Jewish woman's role provides an advantageous model for contemporary women, and the need to affirm her case is because of contemporary confusion over women's place in society. This means that he admits that feminism has induced the need to defend the traditional role of Jewish women. Miller's defense is relatively superficial, because he does not address specific feminist arguments, but brave in that he confronts the most drudging and maligned aspects of woman's fundamental role of motherhood. He expounds on the value of woman's functioning in her unique feminine capacity, as opposed to defenses that tend to heroicize the atypical Jewish woman who has achieved success in areas usually dominated by men, such as business and scholarship. The thrust of Miller's argument is that the Jewish woman does not have to be different to be great, that if she does nothing else but bear and raise a child in the Torah tradition, she is realizing the feminine potential of her people. Thus his seeming heroification of the Jewish mother is simultaneously a statement of the significance of motherhood and of Torah education in Judaism.

Miller writes:

> We have forgotten.
> We have forgotten that the miracle of bearing children is nothing less than entering into a partnership with G-d (Talmud, *Nidda* 31a).
> We have forgotten the joyous wonder of the first mother, Chava (Eve): "I, together with G-d, have made a man!" (*Bereishis*/Genesis 4:1).
> We have forgotten how the Torah, depicting our relationship with Hashem, describes it by a Divine metaphor of mother and child, with the whole Jewish nation portrayed in the role of the loving mother (Talmud, *Ta'anis* 26b and Rashi).
> We have forgotten who we are, even what our physical selves are. The genes within us are the legacy of generations of saintly ancestors, and we have the sacred privilege of passing on to our children the chromosomes of Abraham and Sarah. Each baby is another link, and a step closer to the arrival of Moshiach [Redeemer, lit. Messiah]:

"The Son of David will not come until all the souls are born" (Talmud, *Yevamos* 62a).

Once we begin to remember, does there remain any need to "justify" a career of motherhood, or to feel apologetic for the blessing of a large family?[61]

Shoshana Pantel Zolty's statement of self-affirmation is more daring than Miller's and some of the other defenders of the ultra–Orthodox Jewish woman, such as Moshe Meiselman and Menachem M. Brayer. *"And All Your Children Shall Be Learned": Women and the Study of Torah in Jewish Law and History* is a painstakingly researched study of the legal and social history of Jewish women's education. Zolty attempts to dispel the myths about women's halakhic and historic exclusion from Torah study. Her research is both prescriptive and descriptive of women in Torah study, traditionally the lifeblood of Judaism. She does not diminish the importance of women's centrality in the building of the Jewish home, nor does she diminish the importance of the home as a real center of Jewish continuity. But she does make the claim that women legally can and historically have contributed to that other bastion of Jewish continuity, Torah study. Her thesis asserts that this participation does not exceed the bounds of Jewish law, and, historically, devout and determined ultra–Orthodox women have exercised their prerogatives out of a sincere love of Torah.

Zolty's legal and historical analysis is intricate and expansive. But its greatest contribution to our understanding of the play of cultural tensions in the Jewish world is the statement it makes about how a defense of the ultra–Orthodox woman may look, the extent to which feminist thought has influenced but is also critiqued by the advocates of traditional Judaism.

Zolty is not interested in defending traditional society as it exists simply because it exists. She breaks away from other religious critics by examining not only what the status of women is, but what it might be. She writes that "we should recognize the gap that often exists between the ideal and social reality, between the *Halakhah* and life itself.... What often troubles some women are actually insensitive actions or remarks that are foreign to authentic Jewish tradition."[62] There is a subtle criticism of the ultra Orthodox status quo implicit in her arguments. She follows the lead of Jewish feminism in choosing to focus on a male-dominated aspect of Jewish life that has been given much negative attention by feminism. Thus, we can assume that Zolty is respectful of the concerns that Jewish feminism has raised. Her research frequently agrees with and mentions the observations of feminists, including Rachel Biale, Blu Greenberg, Debra Renee Kaufman and others.

However, unlike Jewish feminists, Zolty is careful to attribute the validity of women's participation in all areas of Torah study to its legitimization within the bounds of Jewish law. Thus, the meticulousness of her halakhic analysis demonstrates a respect for the inviolability of Jewish law. Similarly, her historical analysis of prominent, learned, Torah-observant women denies Jewish feminism the stereotypes of ignorant, excluded, traditional women on which its censure is based. Her research makes a positive declaration of the Torah's flexible support for women's study of sacred texts, even in times and places that did not value education for women. Zolty reaffirms the Jewish woman's capacity as mother, as teacher of Torah to her children and as Torah scholar in her own right.

Showcasing the Thinking Woman

We will hear the voice that reaffirms traditional Jewish women throughout much of ultra–Orthodox critical literature. But there is a stronger tone of this voice in some of the literature; a certain strain that is actually designed to advertise Jewish womanhood to the Jewish woman, to showcase the intellectual and spiritual depth of the ultra–Orthodox woman. This strain of writing is intelligent and analytic, meant to make the ultra–Orthodox woman appreciate the image of her most profound self within the mirror of traditional Judaism. Its theme is the "thinking woman," and it implies that the only reason the Jewish woman has not found her identity in Torah Judaism is because she has not stopped to think about it. If she would examine the role of women in traditional Judaism, she would understand how fulfilling it is. Thinking women, professional and academic, who have taken on religious practice are held up as examples. They form a bridge of communication between ultra–Orthodox Jewish women and thinking, secular-but-searching Jewish women.

The message is that if these professional and academic women, who are successful according to mainstream, secular standards (and often young, pretty, bewigged, not to mention thin, in the pictures) can find their feminine/spiritual/emotional/intellectual fulfillment in traditional Judaism, then so can you. This cogent, charismatic type of critical writing — of which there is as much, if not more, written by men as by women — tends to showcase the intelligent women who have made a successful link between the secular world and the religious one. These women are the subject and often the writers, using the academic forms of their former training to now analyze and display the power of the Torah and its place in women's lives.

Wellsprings: A Quarterly Journal Exploring the Inner Dimensions of Torah and Jewish Life, for example, often displays an ultra–Orthodox women's showcase. Much care has been placed in the aesthetic production of the journal, which is not surprising considering that it is published by the Lubavitch Youth Organization, whose focus is on reaching out to Jews who have little knowledge of Judaism. A positive, professional presentation is part of the outreach. Another part of it, or a result of it, is an acceptance, even an appreciation of certain secular models, which other ultra–Orthodox groups do not appreciate to the same extent. For example, secular academic achievements are greatly valued in outreach literature. College degrees mean something, and women's voices are well represented. This is in keeping with the theme of the thinking woman as a bridge between the world of traditional Judaism and the "outside" world. The contributing writers are usually academics speaking about traditional Judaism, with their academic, secular achievements displayed and honored.

One photo essay in *Wellsprings* features women who are exploring and returning to traditional Judaism. The first line of the biographical blurbs lists the women's academic degrees and fields of study.[63] Another biographical photo essay features women discussing their visions of themselves as Hasidic women. The subtitles in the article are imitative of feminist dialectics, including phrases such as "women's voices," "transcending gender," "expanding horizons," "shattering consciousness" and "chasidic feminist."[64] Many of the women featured in this article were raised in secular homes and adopted traditional practice in young adulthood. The philosophical tone of their musings is representative of the overall tone of the journal, which advertises itself as "a synergy of Jewish ideals and contemporary ideas ... from

Freud to feminism, from Kafka to Kabbalah ... to get you think-ing."[65]

These two biographical photo essays in *Wellsprings* form an inter-esting contrast to the commercial photo books about Hasidim that Jack Kugelmass reviews.[66] He demonstrates that the photographic images of Hasidim and the text accompanying the photographs, if there is any, function in various ways to recuperate the memory and image of the Hasid as a "Jewish icon." He concludes that each of the photo books set up, or "iconize," the black-clad, Old World Jew as "other" to the contemporary Jewish American reader. The photographer presents Hasidim as an idea, a relic or the essence of Jewish identity.

This constructed image of the Hasid operates in two ways: The Hasid represents the essence of Jewish American cultural distinctive-ness, which means that the otherness of the Hasidim merges into the otherness of Jews as a whole. Or, the image of the Hasid represents a radical, different Jewish self to which the American Jewish self as a whole feels otherness. In general, these commercial photo books posit intercultural differences between Jews. Depending on the book, the reader may feel more or less of an affinity or repulsion to the Jews in the pictures. But the relationship is based on the Hasidic Jew as other to Jewish American identity, as either its romantic, uncorrupted, essential self, or as its black-garbed, ritual-focused self. The two con-structions of otherness come together in the construction of a united self as other: Hasidim, in their difference from other Jews, remind all Jews of their Jewish difference.

If secular Jewish photo books set up Hasidim as a different cul-tural group within Jewry as a whole, the photo essays in *Wellsprings* are intended to serve the opposite purpose. These Hasidic women seem to be saying, "We're not so different from you after all." The prominent reiteration of worldly achievements plus the friendly, open faces in the pictures seek to break down barriers of intercultural oth-erness between Jews. The women featured in the photographs invite us to examine their perspective from their side of the fence. Yet this very gesture acknowledges and therefore reinforces the existence of difference between contemporary Jewish American identity and ultra–Orthodox Jewish identity.

Aura: A Reader on Jewish Womanhood is another attractive Lubav-itch publication that showcases Judaism and the women who practice it to the thinking reader. This book is an anthology of critical essays by religious men and women, most of them academically oriented, published writers. It opens with an eloquent self-portrait by a thinking woman, a medical doctor who became religious, and documents her personal spiritual search. She poignantly describes the synthesis between empirical and intuitive knowledge that drove her to seek a meaningful, spiritually based framework for her life:

> Then, while gazing at a diagram I had made depicting the various organs and the changes in them throughout the monthly cycle, I suddenly realized: all this is utterly miraculous. These chemical agents which travel in the blood, bringing instructions to their target cells, and causing vast changes in them — in the ovary, where a follicle ripens, and an ovum is released ... how phenomenal it all is! It's a sublime symphony, I realized, following some unacknowledged celestial conductor.
>
> But one can get high on endocrine physiology for only so long. I was bothered by the inconsistency: an awe-inspiring physical entity whose owner lives a unidimensional, haphazard existence.... I struggled with a persistent dilemma: an exciting and lucrative career, close friends, and trips to the Caribbean, and still my life seemed like a string of platitudes. Science did not — could not — address itself to this issue, and once again my shelves filled with philosophy books. I read extensively and was deeply affected by the writings of Aurobindo, Gurdjieff, and Kierkegaard.... I was disconnected inside. From where would the remedy come?[67]

The above personal exposé is placed side by side with dynamic theoretical explanations of family purity (*mikvah*) laws, candle lighting, prayer, having children, any area, practical or abstract, that is relevant to the religious Jewish woman. *Aura: A Reader on Jewish Womanhood* makes a strong statement about the gravity of the ultra–Orthodox woman's position and is meant to counteract popular stereotypes about her subservience, powerlessness and unimportance in Jewish life.

Rabbi Heschel Greenberg in *Aura* states that his article is an attempt to respond to the challenge, "Why were women not given the same number of responsibilities as men?" This challenge refers to women's exemption from time-related positive Torah commandments, which has done much in shaping women's home-based role in Jewish life. His approach is based on Torah authorities who assert that "women are endowed by the Almighty with a greater measure of natural sensitivity towards matters of the spirit. The degree of refinement and purity a man can attain only through the observance of the time-related commandments is given to women from birth."[68] H. Greenberg, by conceptualizing the commandments as a vehicle for spiritual purification, refutes the "facile conclusion that women are considered second-class Jews."[69] He insists that judging women's status based on the number of commandments they are required to perform is a misunderstanding of the purpose of the commandments.[70]

Greenberg's essay is representative of the critical reaffirmation of the ultra–Orthodox Jewish woman's role that we see throughout the literature. The reader hears the author's argument, but we are not invited to hear a direct examination of the opponents' case. Mainstream Jewish feminism lurks as some vague challenge, which sets the focus of critical ultra–Orthodox writing on the reaffirmation, reexamination and promotion of the Jewish woman. But the opponent — mainstream Jewish feminism — is not invited into the ring, so to speak.

Another example is Susan Handelman's scholarly study "Niddah and Mikvah — A Chasidic Approach," an analysis of the Jewish concept of *niddah*, menstrual ritual impurity, which responds to feminist attacks on traditional ideas of ritual impurity regarding women. However, feminist arguments are not directly challenged but form a backdrop of opposition. Handelman's essay does not defend traditional Judaism by challenging feminist arguments but by providing a deeper understanding of one aspect of Torah consciousness regarding women. In the following passage, we can see how Handelman challenges feminist opposition to ultra–Orthodoxy but only indirectly by way of her subject's analysis.

> We must distinguish, then, between two types of *tumah* [ritual impurity], two types of absence of holiness, two types of "descent." There is the *tumah* that we ourselves create when we intentionally push God's presence away and create a void, thus increasing the darkness and lowly state of the world; and there is the *tumah* that God, so to speak, creates as a part of nature, whose purpose is to enable us to bring ourselves and the world to a higher level, to ultimately reveal more light, more Godliness. This distinction is crucial to our understanding of *niddah* [menstrual impurity]. The *tumah*, the impurity that attaches to a sin is a void *we* create, and by which

we degrade ourselves. The *tumah* of *niddah*, however, is a built-in part of a woman's natural monthly cycle: her "descent" from a peak level of potential *kedushah* [holiness] (i.e., where a life is possible) does not mean that she is, God forbid, "sinful" or "degraded," "inferior" or "stigmatized." On the contrary, precisely because there is such a great level of *kedushah* involved in woman's possession of the Godly power to create — as if *ex nihilo*— a new life within her body, there is the possibility for greater *tumah*— but also a great elevation.[71]

Handelman hints that her argument responds to the criticism that Jewish impurity laws brand women "sinful," "degraded," "inferior" or "stigmatized." She does not tell us exactly who her opponents are, who said the words in the quotes. Neither does she present or refute their arguments in full. This does not seem to be the point. The point is rather to explain an area of traditional Judaism that has been maligned and misunderstood, not to explain the arguments of those who have maligned and misunderstood it. An awareness of Jewish feminist dialectics is assumed.

Canonizing Her-story

As we have seen, a part of the self-affirming aspect of ultra–Orthodox critical literature is the display of outstanding women. Self-portraits act as showcases for their writers' personalities and experiences, and we will see many self-portraits in ultra–Orthodox women's literature. But in several works, including the journal *Wellsprings*, we also see a literal listing of religious Jewish women. The books of Shoshana Pantel Zolty, Tamar Frankiel and Michael Kaufman all showcase important, Torah-practicing women, models for emulation by the Jewish women these authors address. We find extensive inventories of historically important female figures, remarkable for the statement they make about the fundamental needs of ultra–Orthodox critical writing.

The fact that Zolty, Frankiel and Kaufman all devote significant chunks of text in their groundbreaking works to describing the lives and deeds of outstanding religious women is significant. It means that critical advocacy for ultra–Orthodox Jewish women is starting at ground level, the bottom. The basic self-worth of the religious woman must first be historically proven, documented and categorized, before corrections in or defenses of her model can be theorized. Thus showcasing, actually documenting, the important women of the past serves to create an official history of the ultra–Orthodox woman. This is a profound statement of self-affirmation. The literary activity of showcasing thinking women and righteous women culminates in the canonization of an official history for her and ripples throughout the literature as a validation of her present.

This canonization of historical ultra–Orthodox women models — the formalization of "great Torah-observant women" as a category — was one of the early critical moves made by ultra–Orthodox literature. In 1980, S. Feldbrand published a short, innovative book that briefly reviewed the historical contributions of Jewish women from the times of the Talmud, approximately two millennia ago, to the present.[72]

While feminists had been searching for models of female power, feminist models could not consistently emulate the values that were crucial in an ultra–Orthodox Jewish heroine. Feldbrand's *From Sarah to Sarah* clearly attempts to demonstrate that there is an abundance of important and talented Jewish women throughout history who were dedicated to traditional Judaism if not Jewish leaders themselves. *From Sarah to Sarah* introduces models for ultra–Orthodox women and serves to counteract feminist complaints of women's invisibility and unimportance in Jewish history. The extremely positive, uncritical tone of Feldbrand's descriptions makes clear that she intends to confer heroic status upon the religious women's community more than she intends a cool, disinterested examination of history. On the other hand, the brevity of her descriptions proscribes critical fantasy and seems to ensure that she stays within the bounds of the sourced facts.

Ultra-Orthodox writers obviously feel that the canonization of women's models is a necessary first step that grants them the validity, the voice, to speak in the present; to speak against their ideological detractors and to speak critically about themselves. Ultra-Orthodox critical writing, though late in coming, has written the Jewish woman — functioning in her many capacities as a traditional Jew — back into history. This, too, is a rejoinder to Jewish feminism, which has claimed that women have been "written out of history" but which has not

written them "into history" or consistently validated their most typical roles (i.e., as Torah-observant mothers and caretakers) as well as
their heroic roles, such as pious Jewish scholars or martyrs.

In Jewish feminist literature in general, Jewish women in history
are valued for their ability to emulate behavior that is associated with
men. They may verbally affirm the influence of Jewish women as life
givers and nurturers within the Jewish community, but the extensive
praise is saved for the women who were atypical, i.e., warriors, scholars and big money makers, whether or not they were good examples
of piety or morality. Jewish women throughout history are praised far
more for their power than their good deeds. This is the thrust of Sondra Henry and Emily Taitz's classic feminist canonization of Jewish
women in history, *Written Out of History: Our Jewish Foremothers.*[73]

Henry and Taitz's book performs the same activity that is performed by many other critics, including ultra–Orthodox critics, to
validate their agendas. Their book, along with many other Jewish
feminist readings of history, depicts the lives of women who have been
invisible and forgotten. As a critical activity, the representation of historical Jewish women is valued by advocates of traditional Judaism as
well. Torah-observant scholar Menachem M. Brayer writes:

> The indifference by historians, psychologists, sociologists, and cul-
> tural exegetes of Jewish life throughout the ages to the enormous
> impact of the Jewish woman on society has resulted in the lamenta-
> ble lacunae on the subject. The cause of this purblindness seems
> clear to me: most literary works and chronicles are the products of
> man's pen — hence, the bias.[74]

Historic Description or Invention?

Combing through history for models that substantiate current
claims of societal importance and self-worth has academic merit but
can be easily misused. Historic grounding quickly becomes historic
invention. Religious writer Shoshana Pantel Zolty scans history in
order to validate her point that women learning Torah is not a phenomenon exclusive to our times. However, her examples of female eru-
dition do not override the general picture of these women scholars'
exceptionality in history. Zolty's research serves as an example of

historic grounding that attempts to substantiate its historical claims without relying on distortion. Zolty takes obvious pains to contextualize historical determinants.

Written Out of History, however, makes imaginative leaps based on its research. Henry and Taitz often propose simplistic associations and evaluations that clearly support their own agenda but do not always reflect the nuances of historical veracity. For example, they mention the obscure figure of Sarah, a Yemenite Jew who wrote a poem eulogizing the Jewish tribe of Banu Quraiza, which was routed and massacred by Mohammed. For the purpose of smooth literary flow, she is associated with the notorious figure of Kahinah, a warrior who conquered and briefly ruled over the Maghreb region of North Africa. Henry and Taitz quote an old ballad that recalls Kahinah's cruelty to her own people, which contributed to her downfall. They clearly state that "she does not hold an honored place in the hearts of North Africa's Jews, who remember her more for her cruelty than for her bravery."[75] In spite of this statement, she is associated with the Yemenite poet Sarah simply because of their mutual presence in Arabic culture. Henry and Taitz write, "Sarah and Kahinah, in choosing poetry and warfare as their means of self-expression, were choosing activities of high value to their people."[76] This, despite evidence that Kahinah's warfare was not valued by her people.

Her role as a warrior, as a visible woman, as a woman of power is deemed enough of a reason by Henry and Taitz to eulogize her. And Kahinah is not simply "written into history" but eulogized by her further association with other famous Jewish women in history. These associations draw on common bonds of warfare while whitewashing the differences, which are far more evident: "Although poetry was by far the more accepted calling, Kahinah was not alone among women in choosing the ways of violence. Deborah the prophetess was involved in warfare, as were other Biblical women such as Ya-el ... and Judith."[77] Henry and Taitz defend their historic grounding of the figure of Kahinah by performing a further, questionable historic grounding. A character like Kahinah is defended, her bloodthirsty reputation vindicated, in order to not only place her in history but to memorialize her. And why? Simply because she was a woman of power, and male-styled power exhibited in women was a feminist rallying point when *Written Out of History* was first published in 1978. The depiction of Kahinah not only forcibly heroicized a woman who should have remained infamous but also demeaned the uniqueness of the archetype of the Jewish heroine. The association of Deborah, Ya-el and Judith with the violence of Kahinah debases the honor and distinction of these Jewish foremothers.

As we have seen in this critique of *Written Out of History*, the activity of historical grounding often misrepresents history as it documents history. The critique shows how ultra–Orthodox scholars also perform a critical activity, which they deem potentially subversive when used by others, although there is, of course, plenty of overlapping in the details of the biographical accounts written by feminist and ultra–Orthodox scholars. It also shows why a canonization of historical female figures by Jewish feminists is not considered to be the last word on the subject, why the publication of *Written Out of History* in 1978 led to the publication of *From Sarah to Sarah* in 1980 and to other Jewish women's history books of this sort later on. Ultra-Orthodox scholars felt the need to present the historic contribution of Jewish women in their own words.

CHAPTER FOUR

Critical Advocacy: Rereading History

Religious women's writing advocates or is at least a natural expression of ultra–Orthodox "feminism" for the benefit of ultra–Orthodox readers. Religious Jewish women writers publish their works through a limited number of publishing houses, which distribute their works almost exclusively to the religious public. These books are not meant for non–Jewish or secular public consumption or scholarly criticism, yet among the ultra–Orthodox population they are extremely popular. New books are frequently published, and usually the only volumes of creative writing on the bookshelves of ultra–Orthodox homes is the literature of religious Jewish writers.

Perhaps because ultra–Orthodoxy has hardly concerned itself with addressing outsiders or formally redressing its detractors, it has never been accompanied by a significant body of writing that is critically or philosophically aggressive. Perhaps the Torah was always seen as enough of a philosophical entity supporting religious women's issues. More likely, the lack of assertive criticism reflects the same quality that we find in ultra–Orthodox women's literature: an inward focus that displays a disinterest in self-justification and the direct redress of mainstream feminist arguments and a preference for creative expression over critical expression.

I count only four volumes written by religious Jewish writers that can be considered direct, critical responses to feminism from within ultra–Orthodoxy. There are other works, written by both men and women, that discuss women's issues and their status in history, tradition and law, and we have looked at some of them. But only four books directly criticize feminism, though their main purpose is to make an affirmative statement about women's position within Orthodox Judaism. A recent book, Leo Levi's *Modern Liberation: A Torah Perspective on Contemporary Lifestyles*, also defends the Jewish woman's traditional role and poignantly resists feminism. His inquiry primarily stresses a fundamental claim: that a lifestyle, especially a family life and marriage, based on traditional Jewish values provides an answer to the ethical/social problems in human relationships that modern liberation movements have not been able to solve or have aggravated.

The Voice of Sarah: Toward a Feminine Spiritual Difference

One volume of criticism that potentially sets out to promote the traditional woman's position is Tamar Frankiel's *The Voice of Sarah: Feminine Spirituality and Traditional Judaism,* which was published in 1990. This book was innovative in its forthright attempt to champion feminine spirituality in Judaism and Jewish women. It presents femininity in Jewish tradition as an ancient source of inspiration and strength that is still effective today. The critical pith of this book is that it offers the Jewish woman an alternative model to feminism while simultaneously imitating the mode of difference criticism popular in the 1990s. It speaks the language of feminism, situating feminine potency, yet it situates that potency in "patriarchal" Judaism.

Frankiel in *The Voice of Sarah* and Michael Kaufman in *The Woman in Jewish Law and Tradition* both devote significant space to describing the deeds and character traits of outstanding Jewish women throughout history. What is unique about this approach is that it is built upon the premise that modernity has little to offer Jewish women. In order to look forward, we must first look back.

In rereading the traditional texts, Frankiel claims that "we can recover feminine dimensions in our stories and traditions" that may have been there all along: "In my view we have not read carefully enough in the Torah, other biblical writings, and the midrash we already have."[78] In this way, reclaiming Jewish femininity becomes a literary act, and this is largely what Frankiel does. She rereads the histories of Sarah, Rivkah (Rebecca), Rachel, Leah, Ruth, Tamar, Esther, Yehudit and other personalities, searching for feminine potency and inspiration — the *Jewish* female difference.

While Frankiel seeks to reclaim Jewish femininity from traditional sources, she does not ignore the reality of Orthodox women today, the discrepancy between what may be or should be and what is. She realizes that the strength and validity of Jewish femininity for Orthodox women has waned from its historical importance. Meaning to imbue traditional Jewish femininity into modern lives, she writes:

> And yet I also sympathize with the bitter pain of many women who feel cheated by the tradition, who grew to adulthood feeling like second-class citizens, not having been given the resources of strength, courage and self-esteem that should be every Jewish woman's birthright.... Some grave deficiencies have developed in the passing on of the tradition.... Repair is not possible simply by giving women the same kind of recognition previously given only to men.... Are we really doing ourselves a service by molding ourselves to these [male] roles?[79]

She insinuates in this passage that mainstream Jewish feminism, with its stress on adopting and adapting male-dominated rituals, is not the answer. It is crucial to recover authentic Jewish models of femininity for emulation. Thus, the beginning of a search for Jewish femininity is a rereading of history.[80]

In explaining the sovereignty and decline of the influence of femininity, Frankiel seeks to "distill what is useful for us today."[81] What that comes to is an understanding of certain generic features that generally comprise the notion of Jewish femininity. For example, in explaining the decline of women's influence on traditional life, she points to the historical decline of prophecy:

> The significance of these developments is that once prophecy declined in relation to other forms of influence and leadership, women were effectively excluded from the public realm. Neither priest, king, nor law court official was female. By the time of the destruction of the Second Temple, there was no Jewish king, and the priesthood no longer functioned; that left the men of the law courts, who passed on the teachings of the Torah, namely, the rabbis.[82]

What Frankiel wants to distill from her historical evaluation is not the understanding that women must become rabbis in order to regain control in Jewish life but that prophecy is historically connected with femininity. She shows this in the lives of the matriarchs who were also prophets. Recovering and assimilating Jewish femininity empowers Jewish women, gives them back their own nature, so to speak. She is concerned with understanding what is essentially feminine in order to imbue the lives of modern women with its vigor. Recovering feminine selfhood is recovering power.

Prophecy is a more inspirational, inner-focused form of religiosity, and it goes on Frankiel's list of the essentials of Jewish women's spiritual nature "as seen through the lenses of our tradition." Based on her rereading of Jewish sources, she actually draws up a list of general characteristics of feminine spirituality:

> prophetic/inspired
> future oriented, with a sense of history and destiny
> focused on real-life experience (e.g., childbirth) and intimate
>   relations (family and kin)
> having own distinctive relationship to G-d
> sexually/sensually based sense of holiness
> sense of power hidden beneath the surface
> risk taking, life saving, redemptive[83]

Her list is useful when we turn to ultra–Orthodox women's literature for it will help us understand the focus of some of the issues, for example, why childbirth and childrearing are such matters of concern and are seen as spiritual challenges. In delineating the femininity of the matriarchs, Frankiel addresses the concerns we find in the literature of religious women today. She continues:

> Many of the characteristics listed have to do with what we might call the earthly — or as feminist theologians put it, the "immanental" — orientation of the feminine. The growth and development of our spirituality comes in daily, even biological, life as much as in extraordinary experiences. Childbirth is the archetypal expression of this.... It is in the struggles and victories of daily life, both her inner life and her external activities, that women's spiritual strengths emerge. This suggests that the feminine spiritual archetype is not necessarily one clear role.... Rather it is a path of development that takes the matter of life as it comes and fashions it, bit by bit into the clarity of purpose and faith that motivated a Yehudit or a Ruth.

> Moreover, our examples show that extraordinary consciousness can develop in the midst of this ordinary life.[84]

Female heroicism, according to Frankiel's model, is a fusion of the sublime, "risk taking" and redeeming with the ordinary and natural. We could sum it up as a sanctification of the mundane. This aspect of feminine spirituality goes hand in hand with another feature on Frankiel's list, namely "having own distinctive relationship to G-d." In ultra–Orthodox women's literature, we see a religious focus on forging a personal relationship with God, as opposed to the more public forms of spirituality practiced by men. Sometimes female heroicism will be aggressive and public, but it usually emphasizes sanctifying the private domain of home and body, so that the focus of religiosity remains inward and organic.

The relevancy of organic feminist criticism to the work of Orthodox Jewish women should now be clear. This criticism shares a common premise with traditional Judaism and may possess the potential to view the literature extending from it with more cultural sympathy.

While Frankiel's work concentrates on delineating the essence of feminine spirituality in history and ritual, she also connects this research with an address to and challenge of mainstream Jewish feminism. (She still professes to be a feminist.) The whole of her book is actually a response to the brand of Jewish feminism that subverts traditional ritual. The Jewish feminists' approach has been to focus attention on the exclusion of women from rituals that are traditionally practiced by men, while Frankiel's goal is to repossess the femininity of female rituals and role models, the Jewish feminine voice. She asks:

> Why is it that our attention has not been directed to our own tradition, where we have stories of great women who have served as inspiration in previous ages? ... We have largely accepted the Christian and post–Christian condemnation of Judaism as a "patriarchal" religion, indeed as the origin of Western "patriarchal consciousness" which is the source of male-dominated culture, oppressive to women. This assessment of Judaism is incorrect.[85]

She addresses general feminist complaints about Judaism. At times she refutes feminist contentions of women's oppression; at times she agrees but argues that the disparity does not exist theologically or historically. It is a product of the infiltration of negative aspects of Western philosophical thought into Judaism, aspects that denigrate women. For example, she writes:

> Some feminists have claimed that while there may be feminine dimensions to Jewish religious life, they are not really valued in Judaism — synagogue, yeshiva, and law court are more important. From an experiential point of view, many women and men within traditional Judaism will affirm that this is simply not so. Torah life is a total way of life, with women's responsibilities just as serious as men's, and equally highly valued. The question perhaps is whether women have appreciated the importance of affirming this dimension of their lives and speaking publicly about it.... It is only in recent times that women involved in traditional practice have begun to break the silence about their experience.[86]

This brings us back to ultra–Orthodox women's literature. Frankiel refers to it as breaking "the silence" about their experience. If we look at it in this light, it affirms the literature as a reaction to feminism, at least in part, because it only breaks the silence in comparison to secular feminism's loudness. Orthodoxy in general has not concerned itself with bombastic retorts. On one hand, we must realize that ultra–Orthodox writers as a whole have chosen not to enter the arena of feminist dialogue. On the other hand, as Frankiel intimates, they are already there.

The Woman in Jewish Law and Tradition: Setting the Record Straight

Michael Kaufman's *The Woman in Jewish Law and Tradition*, published in 1993, develops Frankiel's thesis in a different direction yet follows a similar format. He is less prosaic than Frankiel, and his work is full of the legal, halakhic explanations that her book lacks. He is also candid about his intent to counteract feminist thinking. He is convinced that ignorance or malevolence are responsible for the misinterpretation of the Orthodox Jewish woman's status. The feminist movement is the clear foe:

> The distortion of the image of the Jewish women has served many ideological purposes. Well-meaning theorists have at times accepted

common misconceptions as fact and have succumbed to the rhetoric and social pressure of the contemporary feminist movement. Others intentionally present a skewed picture. For many the advancement of the status of women is to be attained by denigrating Judaism. In short, the general assumption is that women are subjugated in Judaism. It has become an axiom that needs no proof or substantiation.[87]

While Kaufman does not point his finger at feminism in the body of his text, he does formally address it in his introduction. He explains where the rift is.

> Contrary to widespread belief, many of feminism's goals are entirely in accord with traditional Judaism. However, there are central feminist values that stand at opposite poles from Jewish values. In regard to the fair treatment of women, Judaism supports — in fact preceded — feminism in its fight for the fair treatment of women. But it considers many components of mainstream feminist ideology actually socially regressive and harmful to women and society.[88]

Those components of feminist thought, he argues, are the radical, liberal stances taken by early feminism. The focus on the self in feminism is viewed as antithetical to the God-centered focus in Judaism. Even more threatening to ultra–Orthodoxy are the ramifications of self-directedness on the family, a foundation of Jewish life. Kaufman reveals how the ultra–Orthodox world understands feminism's perspectives:

> The family was perceived as an institution of confinement and restriction for the woman and, furthermore, as an instrument for an oppressive Jewish patriarchy.... Self-development was promoted as a higher value than family or Jewish continuity. Such an ideology is incongruous with the Jewish value system. At Judaism's core is the development of an other-directed consciousness.[89]
> While there is a general awareness of the importance of the Jewish family as a social institution, few appreciate its centrality and even fewer that home and family are far more important than synagogue and temple. It is paradoxical that the glorification of the public sphere and the deprecation of the private sphere is shared by both male chauvinist sexists and many feminists.[90]

The Woman in Jewish Law and Tradition is also a general advocate of the ultra–Orthodox woman's position. Kaufman takes a more halakhic approach than Frankiel, seeking to defuse the myths about women's suppression by showing how Jewish law has been falsely interpreted. He, as Frankiel and Zolty, spends a large chunk of his book reviewing the historical contributions of Jewish women.

> Far from holding a marginal place in Judaism, women have had an extensive impact on Jewish history, to a degree unknown in other cultures. Their influence on the direction taken by the Jewish people has been immense and incalculable and has characterized every age in which Jews have lived. From the biblical period to modern times, it would be no exaggeration to say that Jewish women have shaped the Jewish experience.[91]

He means to assert that the Jewish woman has a voice in Jewish life. The only weakness in his assertion is that many of his examples are outstanding women who are exceptions to the rule. Upholding the handful of women throughout Jewish history who were Talmudic geniuses or religious ascetics contradicts the view of the godliness inherent in fundamental female roles, such as motherhood. In this way, he steps in the path trodden by feminists Henry and Taitz in *Written Out of History*.

Frankiel focuses more on showing how Judaism glorifies the typical and mundane aspects of womanhood. She is also less concerned than Kaufman with justifying the Jewish woman's historical role. She is more concerned with forging a new model for the contemporary Jewish woman based on Jewish history. His goal in rereading history is to cleanse the past of false interpretations. Her goal in rereading is to capture an essential femininity from Jewish sources as a model for the contemporary woman.

But Kaufman also maintains that the modern Jewish woman needs to recapture her essential femininity. For him, this is also largely a reading process. She must research Jewish tradition and law: "Once she acquires a Jewish knowledge, the Jewish woman can apply herself to the discovery of her essential femininity, her feminine spirituality, and her Jewish heritage."[92] This explains why the focus of his book is law and tradition.

One of the strong points of Kaufman's book is that his attack on feminism seems respectful and sincere, allowing feminist thought to spark a certain amount of Jewish introspection. Part of this introspection is the acknowledgment that essentialist feminist criticism unites with traditional Judaism in its goal to define, recapture and celebrate an integral femininity. In order to create this utopian union of essentialist feminism and traditional Judaism, Kaufman focuses on the most basic theoretical correlation between the two. He skims above the conflicting details in the two schools of thought and draws a limited, quixotic, but not illusory, parallel.

> The woman as Jew and the Jew as woman is a powerful being, potentially capable of achieving the transformation of society.... Such a redefinition of society's values leads to the subordination of the individualist, competitive prototype and to the development of a new model whose center of gravity is care and nurturance and that possesses a rich moral dimension encompassing goodness, truth, sensitivity, compassion, and interdependence. The feminalist [essentialist] school of feminist theory speaks of recasting society and creating a better, more compassionate world. Their inspired, transformative dream shares a transcendent vision with Judaism.[93]

To Be a Jewish Woman:
Repudiating Apologetics

Lisa Aiken's *To Be a Jewish Woman* is similar in purpose and style to Kaufman's *The Woman in Jewish Law and Tradition*. Her book also shares a common bond with Frankiel's *The Voice of Sarah* in that they both straddle two literary categories, a relatively uncommon feat. Their books can be included in the list of ultra–Orthodox Jewish women's writing we describe, yet they are also uncommonly self-aware, self-critical and academic. For the purposes of this study, their books are both primary and secondary sources: Frankiel and Aiken as observant Jews are at once the observers and the observed; critic and subject.

The most prominent feature of Aiken's work is its nonapologeticism; its attitude that Judaism is a system that does not need to measure up to foreign standards. She attempts to present an uncorrupted view of women's issues in Judaism. She rejects the portrayal of traditional Judaism according to an agenda of concerns. She claims that Judaism is a system that must be judged experientially on its own terms, and that in order to do so we must realize that it may not satisfy the expectations of contemporary Western culture. In this way, her posture of renunciation is completely opposed to the self-affirming, "showcasing" literature we have reviewed, which respects certain secular standards and even imitates them in an attempt to reach out to non–Orthodox society. Aiken refuses to compromise Judaism or sanction Western culture. She writes:

> We live in a society of instant gratification, where hard work and waiting often seem anachronistic.... Secular democratic societies promote the importance of having rights....
>
> In many ways, it is hard for Torah-observant Judaism to compete with the secular world on the secular world's terms.... Observant Judaism promises no instant gratification, no easy highs, no guaranteed emotional or financial outcomes. Nor does it teach that we are entitled to rights simply by virtue of being alive. We have rights because we were created in the image of God and have accepted His moral obligations upon ourselves.[94]

Aiken responds to modern culture by calling for long-term moral development over short-term, self-seeking pleasures, for meaningful religiosity over "quick spiritual fixes."[95] Her espousal of traditional Judaism has a grim, duty-oriented quality. She reiterates that the Jewish woman can find self-fulfillment in traditional Judaism, but the impact of that assertion is outweighed by her implication that self-fulfillment cannot be the Jewish woman's primary ambition; more important is the fulfillment of her divine obligations. Therefore, in the attempt to unequivocally set Judaism's record straight concerning women's issues, Aiken focuses more on what women do in Judaism than what Judaism does for women. Aiken discusses laws related to women and women's practices at least as much as she discusses the benefits of those practices, which she values mostly in their fostering a durable spiritual growth. Hers is a response not only to Jewish feminism but to modern-day ethical secularism. Her book is a fundamental rejection of the contemporary Western obsession with individualist, sensualist gratification. It is an advocacy of Judaism as an alternative system, as a meaningful, ethical, albeit rigorous, spiritual code.

Aiken's *To Be a Jewish Woman* proposes that Judaism offers a different conceptual framework, that there are fundamental conceptual conflicts between Jewish and feminist consciousness. The advantage of Aiken's nonapologeticism is the boldness we see in her presentation of touchy issues, issues that have undergone feminist scrutiny. Neither does she suppress philosophical and legal aspects of Judaism that seem to promote the feminist agenda. Her book, while clearly written by an advocate of traditional Judaism, is not a stubborn promotion of her own convictions but rather an honest bid for scholarship and clarity.

The result is that Aiken, like Michael Kaufman, does not outrightly aim to reject feminism. She focuses on the women's issues at hand, determined to debunk the myths that have clouded understanding of either the practice or intention of Jewish law and custom. The result is that her explanations of Judaism may sometimes line up with feminism, either partially or completely. Or, more often, her explanations invalidate feminism's very foundations. For example, Aiken's dismissal of motherhood as the only vehicle of feminine expression would probably reverberate well in feminist camps. She writes:

> Women were created with the potential of imitating God in the two greatest ways possible — by creating new life and by giving of themselves in the development and nurturing of others. As is well known, Judaism values women's ability to bear, nurture, and raise children. It also stresses how important it is for them to be stabilizing forces in their husbands' and children's development. Yet, despite Judaism's preference that women marry and have children, men are the ones who are commanded to marry and to procreate, not women [Rashi on *Kiddushin* 35a]. The preferred role for women is to marry and have children, but Jewish law does not require this of them. Should a woman not be able to, or not wish to develop her potentials as a mother, she still has many other ways of imitating God and actualizing herself as a Jewess.... This is not the case for a man, for whom Judaism proposes that he can never fully actualize himself without being married and having children.[96]

Yet, she shatters basic feminist conceptual foundations when she answers the question, "Who has ultimate control over women's bodies?"[97]

> Many secular people feel that abortions should be allowed at the discretion of a pregnant woman, insofar as only her body is affected by carrying a child. This view reflects a premise that a woman's body belongs to her and that she should therefore have ultimate say over what happens to it.

Judaism takes issue with this premise. The Torah tells us that men and women were created in God's image and we do not "own" our bodies. We are the proprietors of bodies that were given to us in safekeeping until such time as God decides to revoke our lives....

People often seek validation of their needs and rights. In Judaism, when people have rights, we also have corresponding obligations. Judaism does not believe that everyone has the right to be sexually active.... Unless there are valid reasons for a woman to use birth control, one of the responsibilities of sex is the possibility of creating a new life.[98]

Feminism and Judaism: Sparring with Feminism

Together, the books of Lisa Aiken, Tamar Frankiel and Michael Kaufman form a groundbreaking attempt to engage in a justification and espousal of the traditional Jewish woman's position. These scholarly books are the closest that traditional advocates have come to a direct response to mainstream Jewish feminism. They also signify that if ultra–Orthodox "feminism" is slowly producing a body of representative criticism, it may yet produce a body of *literary* criticism along with its already-burgeoning body of literature. To my knowledge, this study is the only research to date of ultra–Orthodox women's literature.

In terms of critical development, it is interesting to note the intertextual dialogue in Michael Kaufman's books. Kaufman, who published after Frankiel, makes several detailed references to that author and scholar, to her text and her person, according them both great respect.

Thus far in our discussion we have looked at books that represent a new order in ultra–Orthodox critical writing; books that aggressively defend the ultra–Orthodox Jewish woman. These books, however, are less penetrating in their criticism of feminism. As of this writing, there is only one book that attempts a detailed, in-depth examination of feminism versus Judaism: Michael Kaufman's *Feminism and Judaism: Women, Tradition, and the Women's Movement*, published in 1996.

Feminism and Judaism is an elaboration of the ideas presented in the introduction to Kaufman's *The Woman in Jewish Law and Tradition*. What makes *Feminism and Judaism* such a singular contribution to ultra–Orthodox criticism is that it is an issue-for-issue examination of and direct response to Jewish feminism. The three critical books that we have discussed, and some others, all redress general feminist charges against traditional Judaism. *Feminism and Judaism* goes further by evaluating the feminist literature itself and redressing its specific criticisms. For example, Kaufman formulates a detailed response to the sort of fluid, anti-structure Jewish feminist theology espoused by Judith Plaskow in *Standing Again at Sinai*; he discusses Blu Greenberg's brand of Orthodox-based Jewish feminism; and he recognizes the disillusion of some new-generation feminists with Betty Friedan's *The Feminine Mystique*.[99]

Feminism and Judaism is an answer to the question originally posed by a Jewish feminist: "Are feminism and Judaism at some points ideologically irreconcilable?"[100] Kaufman examines the history of mainstream feminism, Jewish feminism, women in Judaism and even the scientific research on gender differences. He formulates the current ideological position of each faction, delineating the specific points at which feminism is irreconcilable and reconcilable with Judaism. Based on this analysis, Kaufman draws up a model of the "new Jewish woman," the woman who has incorporated feminist consciousness into a traditional Jewish framework. "Discovering her true feminine spirit and the true role of women in Judaism, a Jewish woman at the same time discovers her responsibilities to herself, to her people, and to society."[101]

Who is Kaufman's "new Jewish woman"? Simply stated, she is herself. However, the implementation of this model of the self is not so simple: Defining and manifesting the Jewish female self is a complicated affair after decades of feminist interpretation. The Jewish woman must first rediscover who she is and what is her true nature. She must repossess the best part of herself, the giving part of herself. *Feminism and Judaism* concludes that rediscovering women's innate essence as mother is the key to repossessing the self.

Kaufman shows that it is the mother whom equal-opportunity feminism denigrated, and it is the nurturing qualities of the mother that essentialist feminism lauds. Here *Feminism and Judaism* pinpoints the parting paths between the two institutions, Judaism and feminism.

In liberal feminism's blurring of gender differences — and the sexual revolution it led to — it is irreconcilable with traditional Judaism. Kaufman explains:

> In Judaism gender differences are fundamental; men and women differ in their basic natures, personality traits, and abilities. A movement which insists that men and women be treated equally and that women must suffer in order to uphold this principle cannot be in consonance with Judaism. Nor can Judaism accept a movement that is — even moderately — anti-male, anti-child, anti-family, anti-feminine, or anti-altruism. Such an ideology is inconsistent with values central to the Jewish people.[102]

In *Feminism and Judaism*, Kaufman discusses his thesis that essentialist feminism picks up where mainstream, liberal feminism parts ways with Judaism. In asserting that essentialist, or difference, feminism is largely compatible with Judaism, he states that both these schools share the belief that when

> values and ideals such as caring, compassion, sympathy, harmony, mutuality, love, and a commitment to nurturing life are adopted by society women will also cease to look upon their femininity as an impediment, and cease to seek to emulate men in order to escape from their femininity — but will understand their feminine potential. This is the feminalist [essentialist feminist] ideal — that women will transform the world of conflict, strife, and contentious rivalry, and remake society in a softer mold, into a caring, humane community. *Humanity will progress not when women adopt more masculine values and attitudes, but when men adopt more feminine values and attitudes.*[103]

Thus, the ideal woman is the best part of herself, and in fulfilling her innermost nature, she transforms the distorted masculinity of the world in which she lives.

Kaufman's emphasis on gender differences as the key to the conflict between feminism and Judaism can be seen in the coining of his own terms for the two feminist schools of thought. "Masculofeminism" is how he refers to mainstream, or equal-opportunity, feminism, which affected the "masculinization of women."[104] "Feminalism" is how he refers to the feminisms that focus on the female difference; he also refers to them as the "feminine manifestation of feminism."[105]

His implication is clear: The goal of women's rights activism has not been the liberation of women but the emulation of men. Equal-opportunity feminists who suckled on the ideological milk of Betty Friedan, Kate Millett and Simone de Beauvoir followed an agenda that was "based upon the hypothesis that women attain their ultimate goal and self-realization by becoming female replications of materialistic man."[106] Kaufman agrees with Suzanne Gordon's assessment that mainstream feminism has produced a contemporary woman who is "a faithful replica of the kind of economic, acquisitive man who has historically denigrated the very skills, values, and activities that have been the substance of women's claims to difference."[107]

The dubbing of equal-opportunity feminism "masculofeminism" is clearly a reproach. And while Kaufman cogently argues that the goal of equal-opportunity feminism was the emulation of men, do its proponents deserve to have their femininity slighted? Or perhaps the term masculofeminism is not derogatory but overly simplistic. The emulation of men and antagonism toward men were repercussions of early feminism's struggle, but wasn't the real goal equal opportunity for women? Is this a masculine endeavor that demeans the women who undertook it? Is wanting equal pay for equal work masculine?

Masculofeminism seems to be a simplistic, if not derogatory, sum- mation of equal-opportunity feminism. At the same time, it is under- standable. It is equal-opportunity feminism that focused its criticism on the inaccessibility of male institutions to women. Male-focused activism led women to emulate the forms they criticized as much as change them. In opposition to this, "feminalism" has focused its atten- tion on those values and institutions that are unique to women but have been unappreciated or denigrated. It might be imprecise to call essentialist, or difference, feminism the "feminine manifestation of feminism," but it is more feminine than equal-opportunity feminism in that it is women-focused, seeking to reassess uniquely feminine perspectives and contributions.

What is important for us, beyond the accuracy of Kaufman's ter- minology, is what his choice of language tells us about how traditional Jews interpret feminism and the implications of that interpretation on the writings of religious women. His terminology implies an under- standing that the world is divided into two clear sexual arenas. This does not mean that actions normally associated with men or women are systematically proscribed for the opposite sex. What it does imply is a basic association of actions and attitudes with one gender or the other. We can glean from this an understanding of Judaism's fairly neat dichotomy of human behavior, and even intangible emotive forces, into masculine and feminine divisions or modes.[108]

Men and women each have distinctive biological makeups, both physical and mental. Kaufman brings the research findings of the social sciences to support this claim, asserting that just as men's and women's physical and psychological worlds are different, their outer worlds — their cultural roles — are different. The societal difference between men and women is not so much a function of social conditioning as it is a result of natural, psychological propensities, God-given differences. Thus, mainstream feminism's challenge of the whole idea of role divisions and gender differences was received by observant Jews as a threat of the worst kind to Judaism's viability. Kaufman writes:

> Gender differentiation in Judaism is based upon the inherent *in*equality of men and women. The roles are complementary, and of equal value. In accordance with nature, each gender is naturally more suited to perform certain tasks than the other, yet members of both sexes stand as equals before God. Men's primary role involves the public, external realm; women's primary role involves the private, internal realm. While sexist men and masculofeminist women have joined forces, devaluating the caregiving activities associated with the private realm and maintaining that only participation in the public realm is of value, Judaism rejects this premise.[109]

Kaufman's arguments well represent traditionalist thinking. Even Zolty, with her advocacy of educational equality between men and women, claims that equal "value" does not preclude role differences. She writes:

> Traditional Jewish thought clearly views the woman as equal to man. The dominant perception, however, is that the woman's role is distinct from the man's. It is basic to the thinking of the rabbis that every creature under the sun has a unique mission to fulfill.[110]

CHAPTER FIVE

The Relational Self

A major feature of the writing of ultra–Orthodox Jewish women, which differentiates it from general women's writing, is that it is dominated by autobiographical, anecdotal, personal narrative, not fiction. And even the fiction of this writing/reading community is possessed by realism and frequently imitates the style of personal narrative.

Josephine Donovan in "The Silence Is Broken" gives a historical overview of the exclusion of women from European literature in the medieval and early modern periods and their subsequent predominance in newly developed fiction genres. Classical canons of language use ensured that women, who were uneducated in the classics, did not participate in literary production. However, the "demise of classical authority was encouraged by the gradual replacement of literary patrons by capitalist booksellers.... They were in fact quite willing to pander to a reading public that was by the turn of the seventeenth century predominantly female."[111]

Women's experience in letter writing, informal memoirs and autobiography was the beginning of the genre of the novel and epistolary fiction, both genres that are preferred by women writers. Their familiarity with the vernacular and their centrality in domestic life led to the creation of these genres, which were not based on traditional canons of writing and were focused on familial, "indoor" experiences.

Donovan explains how a new, plain style of language became popular in the mid-seventeenth century and that one feature of that style was the "loose period." This refers to a mode of writing that endeavored to be completely natural, unpremeditated, unmediated and artless, a spilling over of thoughts on the page.

> Such a stylistic method implies an inductive, empiric logic, appropriate to seventeenth-century European society, which had shifted

toward the experientially verifiable and away from received premises as the source of truth. It also implies a spontaneous, unpracticed quality, which when valued, obviates the necessity for formal rhetorical training. Again, women as cultural outsiders stood to benefit from this kind of stylistic shift.[112]

Thus, the spontaneous personal narrative became identified as a female style. This is helpful in looking at the literature of religious Jewish women. There is both similarity and difference between this literature and general literary history. It is plausible to assert that the predominance of personal narratives in religious Jewish women's writings is a consequence of both a familiarity with domestic, family life and an unfamiliarity with classical Jewish canons.

While today's Jewish women are not excluded from learning classical texts — unlike European women in the seventeenth century — their centrality in family life discourages rigorous book learning of classical Jewish texts that have no practical application. Obscure legal or philosophical discussions, which have no bearing on daily life, are not normally considered important for a Jewish woman to study. Her curriculum focuses on basic Jewish texts, necessary *Halakha* and philosophical texts that bring one to greater understanding and faith. Additionally, while women are not expected to learn for the sake of learning, men are. The study of Torah for its own sake is a religious duty encumbent on Jewish men. The learning of detailed or obscure aspects of Judaism is relegated to secondary importance among women; it is relegated to men.

The care of the family in Judaism is a priority for women and is the domain of Jewish women historically and in our own time. The exemption from studying Torah is partly so that religious women, who often have large families, can focus on the needs of the family. In actuality, most ultra–Orthodox women are involved in significant Torah study. But her exemption from studying for its own sake ensures that, when it comes to a question of religious service through Torah study or family care, it is clear that caring for others comes first.

Thus, personal domestic experience is seen as fertile ground for the religious woman to focus her divine service. This translates into the "spiritual work" of becoming a better caretaker, more efficient, more sensitive to the needs of others. The giving inherent in her domestic experience conforms with Judaism's expectations of the commandments as a whole to transform the natural selfishness of humanity into an other-directedness. Giving is a basic aspect of divine service in Judaism, and the ultra–Orthodox Jewish woman in her roles as wife and mother becomes an expert in learning about giving.

For the religious Jewish woman then, the genre of personal narrative is an appropriate mode of description for her experiences, which are derived from the challenges of everyday life. However, the troubling question remains: Why does the writing of religious Jewish women — with its focus on domestic experience and nonparticipation in much of classical learning — rely so much on personal narratives and nonfiction, while European and American women's writing, based on similar experiences, relies more on fiction?

It may be that the development of fictive genres in ultra–Orthodox Jewish women's literature is yet to come. And if so, that development would have its historical precedent in the history of general women's literature. But a more satisfying answer probably lies in the identity of religious Jewish women and then, deeper, in Orthodox Judaism itself. Here again, an understanding of Jewish culture is necessary.

A possible answer is that Judaism professes that life is a divine gift, and a basic goal of life is to transform its mundane aspects into godliness; to take every circumstance and object in the world and sanctify it by compelling it into divine service. *Tikkun Olam* is the theological term for this fundament, literally, a fixing or perfecting of the world through human, moral efforts. Therefore, the most banal aspects of living have the potential to function in a sacred way, to become sacred, as it were. Real life experience, then, the challenges overcome in the course of living, take on a much higher status. Banality is redefined as potential godliness. The common difficulties of everyday living are the raw material for the making of spirituality. How can fiction compare to the lessons learned from living? Fiction is escapism in this light.

Another answer may be that Judaism, like other codes of morality, has an aversion to untruths. By its nature, fiction has something unappealing: the bitterness of lies. The religious mind feels more comfortable with truth.[113] There may also be an underlying fear in the expression of the imagination to a certain extent, a fear in the letting go that accompanies any venture into fiction. Imaginative art can easily overstep the boundaries of the detailed theological codes in Judaism.

Writing that is grounded by realism is more likely to remain in navigable, "kosher" territory, so to speak. The realism of the familiar landscape of personal narrative invests it with a safeness preferred by ultra–Orthodox sensibilities.

These explanations also help us understand why even the fiction of religious women writers attempts to be utterly true-to-life, and we often see that it imitates nonfictive personal narrative.

The Inscription of the Self

"Women first learned to write about their experiences and about themselves in diaries and letters."[114] This is what the editors of *Women and Language in Literature and Society* tell us; which is to say that the writing of personal narrative is as much a search for identity as a search for a descriptive mode.

Michel Beaujour underlines the search for and expression of identity as the most central issue in the autobiographical mode. Can an author succeed in describing herself? Can we trust her own expression or must we read between the lines? Beaujour writes that any self-portrayal is an attempt to deny rhetoric, that is, persuasion by literary strategies. The author's desire is that the self issues forth without any hindrances. But what critics and authors know is that a literary revelation of the self is necessarily bound up with the author's cultural background and subconscious motives. In the attempt to express the self, the author may either subvert the self or rhetorically construct a new self. The writing is a rhetorical production of the self but not necessarily a self-portrait.

> The self-portraitist does not "describe himself" in the way the painter "represents" the face and body he perceives in his mirror: he is forced into a detour ... the self-portraitist never has a clear notion of where he is going, of what he is doing. But his cultural tradition is well aware of it for him: his culture provides him with the ready-made categories that enable him to classify the fragments of his discourse.... At best, the self-portraitist sees in those headings a referential virtuality bound up with the "mimesis of the self."[115]

The conscious writer of a self-portrait realizes that she is giving the reader a construction of herself. We can conclude from Beaujour that the expression of true identity in writing is doomed to fail. The critic looking for the author's true identity in the self-portrait cannot accept the author's image of herself; the critic must search for the inscription of the self within the text. But in what way does the self-portrait succeed?

Beaujour writes, "For the reader, if he has not closed the book again soon after the first page, cannot remain in a third-party position; he has no choice but to place himself in the position of the *addresser* ... each reader of those books can become, in turn, the one who writes them."[116] The popularity of a personal narrative is in its speaking for the reader, telling the reader what *she* has to say, telling her about her own experience. In discussing the most popular personal narratives, we are seeing not only what the ultra–Orthodox woman writer has to tell her readers but what they would say about themselves. "The only true readers of the self-portrait are writers yearning for self-portrayal."[117] The personal narrative is a collective, cultural expression of identity through the writing/reading process. It is the voice of a culture, of the self expressing itself through a culture and of the self expressing the culture. The only self we can attempt to identify is the cultural self and (we may safely add to Beaujour's thesis) the gendered self.

With these limitations in mind, we can seek out those aspects that mark the writing of a cultural gender group. For our purposes: Is there a unique quality about the autobiographies/personal narratives of women? Do we also see these qualities in the writings of ultra–Orthodox Jewish women? How are they the same, qualified or different from general women's personal narrative genres? And why?

Relationality

Mary Mason tries to delineate the difference in women's autobiographical writing. She surveys four early representative autobiographies and draws several conclusions.

> The self-discovery of female identity seems to acknowledge the real presence and recognition of another consciousness, and the disclosure of female self is linked to the identification of some "other."

This recognition of another consciousness — and I emphasize recognition of rather than deference to — this grounding of identity through relation to the chosen other, seems ... to enable women to write openly about themselves.[118]

Her conclusions are relevant for us as well. In the writings of religious Jewish women, we will notice a relationality to some other identity, consciousness or institution, which engenders the articulation of selfhood. It is wise to remember Mason's parenthetical remark: recognition is not the same as deference. We may sometimes notice relationality in a dissociation from the "other," and we must examine relationality in the literature of religious Jewish women not only by looking at *with* what the writer chooses to associate but also *from* what she chooses to dissociate. In doing so, it may be possible to discover how this literature is similar to and different from general women's personal narrative and how it dramatizes "self-realization and self-transcendence through the recognition of another."[119]

Carolyn G. Heilbrun agrees that the expression of the self in women's autobiography is grounded in relationality. But she insists that this is only because the female autobiographical voice is reluctant to admit and is apologetic for its power or anger: its "unwomanliness."[120] The writer has power and wit; the literary voice she constructs refutes this. Heilbrun protests the female voice that puts forth the "fiction of female becoming" as opposed to female self-discovery, autonomy and anger. However, she believes that this traditional pattern is changing.[121]

Following Heilbrun's assertions, Beaujour's "problem of identity" is even more aggravated. According to Beaujour, we cannot trust the self-portraitist's construction of her identity; the writer may subvert the self. Heilbrun in effect tells us that *relationality is the subversion*. The woman autobiographer's dependence on some other consciousness for her self-definition is really a subversion of her true powerful or angry self. Relationality, according to Heilbrun, does not reveal the true identity of women. What it does reveal is that women have traditionally felt compelled to hide their true identities behind the fiction of their dependence on a relation to another consciousness.

Heilbrun complicates our understanding of how we "read" the relationality in women's autobiographies. Do we accept relationality as a mode of female self-identification or of self-subversion? Regarding the ultra–Orthodox literature, I believe we should accept relationality at face value, simply as a way in which women identify themselves, because Heilbrun's assertions smack of an early feminist bias that equates relationality with dependence — and dependence with weakness. In the ultra–Orthodox literature, relationality does not usually mean dependence nor does it mean weakness. Relationality is more likely associated with interdependence and interdependence with caring and loving kindness.

Relationality is heralded as the desired norm in ultra–Orthodoxy and a spiritual achievement. Much of Jewish scholarship expounds on the realization of a purposeful interdependence. Anger and power seeking is denigrated, and positive relationality is a goal for both men and women. It is not remarkable that ultra–Orthodox women, who place a spiritual value on caretaking, would identify themselves through their relationships to others.

Heilbrun's assertion that the autobiographical female voice is reluctant to admit her real power or anger suggests Mary Mason's idea of women writers' "grounding of identity through relation to the chosen other," of self-discovery through relationality to another consciousness.[122] Feeling more or less powerful or angry occurs in the context of relationships. The writer feels power or anger in relation to another consciousness. That other consciousness, Heilbrun implies, is male consciousness. However, in ultra–Orthodox women's literature, there is no negativity, and certainly no disassociation from the writer's relation to male consciousness. There is a deliberate complicity with male consciousness alongside a sense of the author's personal power, of her capacity to choose her associations.

The ultra–Orthodox woman autobiographer constructs her identity through a positive connection with male consciousness. In general women's literature, the relation to male consciousness subverts the self, according to Heilbrun. In ultra–Orthodox women's literature, a relation to male consciousness comprises a part of the writer's identity. Her complicity with men and masculine institutions does not seem to compromise her independence or selfhood to a greater extent than membership in any alliance compromises independence.

Ultimate psychological independence is a meaningless term: Who is independent of the limitations imposed by her society, gender, personal and collective history, even her own nature? When we seek to read women's independence and power in her art we are actually looking for evidence of her independence of choice, her power and freedom to choose the ideological framework in which she places herself. When we dictate which framework is subversive and which liberating, we impose our own value system onto that of the writer. Thus, ultra–Orthodox women's personal narratives clearly display the independence of thought that is produced by the writers' mental freedom to choose. However, *what* ideological choice is made may not conform to outside standards of autonomy.

Heilbrun, for example, makes a quick association between relationality to and dependence upon male consciousness, dependence meaning subjugation. If we adopt her correlation, we can read a duplicity in the psychological dynamic of the ultra–Orthodox women's narratives. That is, the ultra–Orthodox woman writer is, to varying degrees, complicit with male consciousness, dependent on male consciousness, even if it is a self-imposed dependence, which is a subversion of the self. Yet, inasmuch as her writing displays her ability to choose the ideological framework within which her consciousness operates, she is independent, displaying her powerful self. Based on the implications of Heilbrun's explication of relationality, we can trace a duality of an autonomous-self/subverted-self in the ultra–Orthodox woman's search for identity.

I suggest that the automatic association of dependence with subjugation is a value-imposed correlation inspired by liberal feminist theory. Dependence, reliance or relation to an ideological matrix *may* be analogous to subjugation, but it can also indicate a value system that places a high priority on relationality. Realistically and historically, we know that a woman's identity that is based on a relation to male consciousness is usually a function of its dependence/subservience to that consciousness. Our society in general clearly places a high value on independence, so dependence on relation easily slides into subjugation. However, ultra–Orthodox Judaism — which is unusually concerned with the maintenance of a positive (inter)dependence — qualifies as an exception to the rule. In this theoretical position, ultra–Orthodox women authors do not demonstrate a duality in their mode of self-discovery but rather a uniform independence and power to choose, even as they choose to identify themselves through a relation to male consciousness. Relationality, ultra–Orthodox consciousness and male ultra–Orthodox consciousness do not carry oppressive implications for ultra–Orthodox women writers. Their search for identity through relationality and complicity with male consciousness does not display a subversion of the female self but only the power to choose their ideological associations. It also is a strong and rarely heard statement of ultra–Orthodox Jewish perceptions that the ultra–Orthodox male consciousness that a woman actively brings into her life is a constructive part of who women are.

Relating to Divinity

Mary Mason writes that a common feature of women's autobiography is that the writer describes herself in dual roles: "a rather more common pattern of women's perception of themselves [is] maintaining two equally demanding identities, worldly and other worldly, both of which, however, are ultimately determined by their relation to the divine."[123]

We see in the writing of religious Jewish women that the author identifies herself in relation to the mundane and to the holy. She sees herself as functioning on these two planes at once. Her challenge is to confront the demands of the mundane world and improve her response to them. Self-improvement, refining her behavior according to the standards prescribed in Jewish sources, is divine service. God is the most fundamental consciousness in relation to which she defines her self. This is a relationality of duality: The writer relates to divinity in her simultaneous roles as a mundane and a holy being.

CHAPTER SIX

Personal Narratives

In 1990, Sarah Shapiro, a religious Jewish woman, published a diary in which she had made entries for three years. Her book, *Growing with My Children*, was widely read among ultra–Orthodox women. Her book is a search for self-development through the challenge of bearing and raising children. Shapiro is a *baalat teshuva*, a "returnee" to traditional Jewish practice who was not raised in a religious home. The challenges she faces are typical for a woman of her background who was not raised in a large family or in a community where having many children was the norm. Shapiro's quest for self-improvement is intense. Her search as a committed Jewish woman for self-identity in the context of ultra–Orthodoxy is passionate. Her writing is insightful and witty, without a lofty style, which it is not meant to have. Yet her search for self-refinement and identity occurs within the very common, mundane situation of running a home and tending her family. Her quest is entirely relational, born and bred out of the challenges of motherhood. Without the interdependence between Shapiro and the other entities in her life, *Growing with My Children* could not have been written. The identity of Shapiro that we see "growing" on the pages is a direct consequence of her relationships.

She decided that she needed help with housework and childcare, and her search for help becomes a search for self-identity. We see Shapiro defining herself in relation to other consciousnesses. She advertises for a mother's helper and interviews several applicants. An austere, critical young woman who applies for the job as helper compels Shapiro to clarify her own identity. She learns to forgive herself for the imperfections of her home, to accept her individuality in the face of the young woman's criticism. This is how she relates, first to an American applicant and then to the critical woman:

The next morning, another young woman named Rebecca came over in response to the ad. An American, nineteen years old, from — of all places — Fairfield, Connecticut! Why, we were cooked virtually in the same pot! In the course of our conversation, I asked her what she thinks about children yelling.

"Oh, well. It happens." With one well-manicured hand she flicked her long, glossy, disobedient brown hair back from her forehead. "My brother and I used to fight all the time."

"And you're friends now?"

She shrugged. "Sure, we're fine now."

"But what if a child yells at his mother? What do you think of that?"

She pouted, casually arched an eyebrow. "Oh, well, I guess it's healthy. To get it out. Even adults have to get it out." How refreshingly American! Our culture's pop psychology. I wish I could swallow it, but if you gulp it down whole, it leaves you half-empty. It's only a fragment of the truth.

Rebecca and I were still talking over our coffee cups when the phone rang. "Is this Sarah Shapiro?" It was that exquisite Italian accent.

"Yes," I murmured. My mind grazed over all the events of the day before.

"Sarah, this is Sonia. I want first to ask you how you feel, if you are all right."

"Yes, Sonia, I'm fine." *She has no idea how much I went through last night because of her [criticism]*, I thought. *She has no idea how much I've learned in just one day on account of her colossal insensitivity and arrogance. I have reaffirmed myself.*

"Well, I would like to say that if you wish, I would like to try being au pair at your house."

I glanced over at Rebecca, who was gazing around the kitchen. I felt like a woman with two suitors. "But ... what about all the things you objected to — that it's not tidy enough, and the children. How —"

"Well, Sarah, I have not been able to sleep all this night, for my worry of what I did to you. And I just pray with all my heart that *HaShem* shall forgive me. They say that you should not judge a person until you are in his shoes, and I do not know — I do not have this experience of being a mother of six kids, so I pray that *HaShem* will one day give me this privilege, to have an untidy house full of noisy children. For that is the blessing, if you can open your eyes to see."[124]

In this passage, we see Shapiro testing the boundaries of her personal ideas about childrearing against those of the two women applying for the job as au pair. She realizes that Western "pop psychology" as expressed in the American girl's flippancy and tolerance for disobedience stands in contrast to her own judgment. Contemporary Western culture is obviously familiar to Shapiro, but she finds it "half-empty." We see that Shapiro perceives Western consciousness, at least in part, as oppositional to her own mentality, and it is this opposition that is responsible in part for the reaffirmation of herself. We will find Western culture the culprit imputed in several women's reexaminations of self-identity.

In a later book, as Shapiro sits on the bed of a friend who is nearing death, she rails against her own inability to grasp the reality of death. She can't help but imagine herself after her friend's death, the actor in her own imagined play, crying over the loss, yet important, too, because she was the last one who had held her friend's hand, the object of others' amazement and talk. She blames her pampered American upbringing for preventing her from fully grasping the reality of death, that this is no shifting surface image, no illusive veneer on life. This is death, the real thing. She thinks:

> what a curse to have started out as a suburban American child! No matter what happens, your roots are in country clubs and academic competitiveness, getting your legs tan, your hair right.... Oh! To be sentenced to such a mentality! No matter how much you hate it, no matter how far away you get in life, nothing ever seems quite real after that, after growing up in that soil. Not even a deathbed.[125]

Shapiro's quest for self-transcendence in the previous passage also includes the quest of Sonia, the young, critical woman (with the "exquisite Italian accent"). The development of these two women is mutually dependent, and there are many such relationships in Shapiro's writing. Female friendship is about helping another in her own personal quest for self-improvement or spiritual self-transcendence and being transformed in the process. Shapiro reaffirms herself by defining her consciousness both against American culture's "pop psychology" and against Sonia's criticism. Sonia's relation to Shapiro opens up an interaction that leads her to condemn a certain aspect of her mentality and affirm a different aspect of it, namely that six kids and a noisy house is a blessing not a liability.

This same personal transformation through relationality is what happens with Shapiro's sister, an accomplished child psychologist, who had always criticized Shapiro for becoming pregnant in such close succession.

> "I hear from Mommy and Daddy that you're pregnant, Sarah," she told me after a minute or so on the long-distance line…. "I've been trying to get pregnant for so long. I'm frightened that I won't be able to because I'm forty-one."
>
> "Oh, Candis, I'm sure that —"
>
> "I'm scared now that I made a mistake to put it off."
>
> "No, really there are a lot of women who get pregnant at that age. They just had to wait a while. A lot of women in Israel have children after forty."
>
> "They do? Really? Their first, though?"
>
> I rummaged through my mind. "Yes, I know two like that."
>
> "Really?"
>
> "Yes. It'll just make you appreciate the baby when it comes."
>
> There was a pause. I assumed that she was concealing the other side of her thoughts now. "Candis," I ventured, "are you mad at me for being pregnant again so fast?"
>
> "No."
>
> I couldn't believe it. "But Candis, Eli is just seven months old. Isn't that ridiculous?"
>
> "No, it'll be all right. A lot of people have children close together, and it's all right. Look at me. Mommy didn't want to have another baby, and look how wonderful I am." We laughed.
>
> "Candis! You really think so? I can't believe you're not mad at me."
>
> "No, I'm jealous."
>
> "*Jealous?*" My astonished heart melted with gratitude….
>
> "Sarah, I'm scared that maybe I'll never have children. It's so hard for me to imagine not ha —"
>
> "No, I'm sure you will. I'm sure of it."
>
> "You think so?"
>
> I resolved to pray, and to ask the children to pray. "Candis, hearing all this from you is so strange for me because I've always felt so inadequate next to your being a doctor —"
>
> "Psychologist."
>
> "Psychologist. The fact that you actually have patients come to you and that you have your own business and do well. And that paper you wrote for the Congressional Committee." Candis was quiet on the other end. "Candis? Did you hear me?"
>
> "Yes. I heard you. I just want to be at home with a baby."[126]

In the course of this conversation, Shapiro's pregnancy intensifies Candis' recognition of her own desire to have a baby and that having a baby is more precious to her than her career. Candis now affirms what she always condemned in her sister and affirms those values in herself. Shapiro found the support she always wanted from the sister she respects and gained an affirmation of a certain part of her way of thinking and living that was previously in opposition to her sister's mentality. Shapiro and her sister strengthen the value of their self-images as mothers through a relation to each other's consciousness.

While we see Shapiro forging her identity in opposition to some of the consciousnesses she confronts, her relation to male consciousness is one of collusion. Her quest for transcendent motherhood takes place within the framework of traditional Judaism; and that quest is never threatened by male-dominated institutions nor by her marriage. There is no concession between her identity as an ultra–Orthodox Jewish woman and her relations to men, male-dominated institutions or male consciousness. The collusion is complete; not only does male consciousness *not* threaten her selfhood, it helps her in her quest. For example, she decides to take the problem of imperfect motherhood to a rabbi, trusting that the rabbi can help her. We can see the author's personal power in her determination to remake her character:

> "My anger, Rav Simcha. I lose my temper with my children and my husband."
>
> "Often?"
>
> I nodded. I was ashamed. "Yes.... I want to change this about myself."
>
> "It is your nature."
>
> My nature? A weight of hopelessness clamped down upon me. "You mean I won't be able to change?"
>
> "Can an apple become a pear?" His black eyes twinkled. "You will have this nature until you die."
>
> Until I die? That couldn't be. It couldn't be that as an old woman I would still just be the same person I am now!
>
> "Your Creator gave you this nature so that you would always have to work to overcome it ... so that you would not be able to forget about Him. If you were always strong and perfect, you would feel that you are the creator of your own talent. It is only your weakness that brings you to an awareness of your Creator."... Getting up abruptly from the table, the rabbi shuffled his feet lightheartedly and swung his arms.

"How can I do this?" he asked. *What in the world was he getting at? How could he do what?* "How is it that I walk? I walk because God gives me the power to walk. How do you walk?" He paused. I sat there, blank. "Because your Father in Heaven gives you the strength to walk. *He also gives you the strength to restrain your temper, to go beyond your nature.* In the moment that you hold yourself back from lashing out, God takes the gr-r-r-eatest pleasure in you."...

"All right, I do think maybe I could succeed sometimes but I know I'll fall back."...

"So you must pick yourself up again. When you fall, do not be broken, and when you succeed, do not be swallowed by pride. God is not in the brokenness nor in the pride."

"But sometimes I do feel so disappointed in myself."

"Who are you to feel disappointed? Did you create yourself?"

A foreign concept. My mouth fell open.

"The sweetness of life," the rabbi said with a wide grin, "is in the true struggle."[127]

Shapiro's husband has a marginal but supportive role in her diary. Yet the challenges she faces in her relationship with him also play a part in her self-development.

The subtle successes Shapiro achieves, such as screaming less at her children, are very significant to her; they are her divine service. This can be seen in the seriousness she places in every aspect of her self-development, in the importance she places on the small things she learns and, more than anything else, in her decision to meet with the rabbi. Her outlook is that raising children with all its grinding drudgery and toil, with its fundamental particulars, such as talking to a child with respect, is godly. Godliness combines commonplace activities with an awareness of the sanctity inherent in them. It is the service of the mind to constantly remind the doer that her mundane activities are, on a different plane of existence, holy.

In the following poem, Shapiro expresses this twofold relation to divinity. Listen to how this dual relationality works through a contracted and then expanded consciousness, how the awareness of the two planes of existence she simultaneously occupies "flashes through her like lightning." She is first possessed by a sudden awareness of God, and then she possesses the awareness, allowing it to lead her to a new realization of her unity with the world — and transcendence.

Washing dishes, watching the dishes,
not really seeing
her hands wash the dishes, because
it's always like this, and the sun
lengthening along the floor.
                              One,
two o'clock, and then she's done
the laundry. Get the baby crying.
Sweet baby.

Because.
There is no because.

But one day the sun hits a frying pan in soapy water
and she's holding a rainbow.
The thought flashes through her like lightning:
"G-d's creating light!" and she sees all this,
the light the water her hands herself
are miracles.[128]

In the next poem, listen not only to how her self-transcendence is based upon the mundane but to how the relations in her life (kids and house) are the starting point for her self-identification and self-transcendence.

It's not to England that I'm traveling.
It's not to France.
It's not to Thailand I am going.

                    I am going
to clean off the stove
and wipe the milk off the fridge. I'm going
I'm on my way
to the emptiness
of the house after the children have left for school,
when I and my coffee cup
will murmur nothing, and we will gaze
at the bright, cloudy blank of the window.

                    Up, up and away
I'm in a hurry. I've said goodbye. I've said so
long!
All by myself, I will be here

in myself, with the refrigerator humming.
I'm letting go. And I shall sail

into my own

it's my very own

whiteness[129]

Behind all of the intense concern with identity and transcendence, behind the female power that is centered in relationality yet does not compromise its selfhood, lies the nagging perception that Shapiro's superconsciousness might be, after all, a defense against early feminism's attack on the very idea that a woman's identity is dependent upon her relations to others. Here is how she opens her book:

> On the cover was a fair-haired, smiling, ethereal-looking lady, enclosed delicately in some sort of mist. The book appeared on the coffee table one Friday when my sister came home from college for the weekend.... I knew my sister had learned from this book, in one of her classes at Sarah Lawrence, that my mother had wasted her life. My mother had been fooled and misused, tricked into sacrificing her potential as a person for the sake of her husband and children. How lucky that at least now, we, the younger generation, could wake up and avoid making the same horrible mistake.
> It was entitled *The Second Sex*. Did that mean that women really were second, or that they really weren't second? I looked at the pretty lady on the cover and wished I looked like her. She was fair and blonde. I was dark. Her gentle, knowing far-away smile hinted that whatever "second" was, she wasn't....
> When my sister went back to college on Sunday, the peace to which she abandoned us was a vague indictment of our plight: stuck at home....
> What had changed, to be more exact, was that [mother's] selflessness had all of a sudden become dishonorable in my eyes. And I thought I could discern in *her* eyes a new, frightened defensiveness: "So maybe I *have* been misused, maybe I *have* given up too much," my mother's expression seemed to say. "But this is my job and I'm going to do it right!"[130]

In this excerpt, Shapiro demonstrates that while she, like her sister, belonged to the "younger generation," she relates more to her mother's position than to her sister's. She identifies more with the Jewish mother's defensiveness than with the feminist offensive. She questions whether or not de Beauvoir's attack could be sincere by asking what she really means by women being second: Are they second or not? It seems to Shapiro that de Beauvoir's accusations reflect the author's exclusivity, that she does not include herself in the group of women she accuses of complicity in male subjugation. If so, de Beauvoir's observations are reserved for a particular type or group of women. Could she really mean that women are second when she herself is a woman? Or, does de Beauvoir's case focus on a biological group from which she exempts herself: "whatever 'second' was, she wasn't." Shapiro's feeling of exclusion from de Beauvoir's charismatic circle of critical privilege is expressed when she says, "I ... wished I looked like her. She was fair and blonde. I was dark." Shapiro seems to say, consciously or not, that it is her Jewishness, her "darkness," that excludes her.[131]

In feeling excluded from enlightened womanhood because of her Jewishness, Shapiro expresses in experiential, impressionistic terms the exclusivity that Elizabeth Spelman finds upon close examination of *The Second Sex*. Spelman writes, "I think that in de Beauvoir's work, we have all the essential ingredients of a feminist account of 'women's lives' that would not conflate 'woman' with a small group of women — namely, white middle-class heterosexual Christian women in Western countries. Yet de Beauvoir ends up producing an account which does just that."[132]

Shapiro's personal narrative, with this opening blurb from her impressions as a young woman, explains how an early work of feminist thought made her feel defensive of motherhood and defensive of Jewishness, how her initial, natural identification was with the Jewish mother, even though she felt compelled to be counted among the group with critical privilege. The potency of feminism as a force to be reckoned with in her life can be seen in Shapiro's presenting it to the reader on the opening page — though it has little to do with the rest of her book. It also explains why the writings of *baalot teshuva* like Shapiro indicate that their early contact with feminism may have them spending the rest of their lives justifying the giving and relationality inherent in their identities as Jewish mothers.

In a different book, Shapiro imputes *The Feminine Mystique* with inspiring certain behavior that she later regretted.[133] In this case, she was prompted to challenge the Jewish mother's giving, namely the giving of her own mother as she catered to her father in the early part of his illness. Her imputation of feminism is no doubt fueled by the guilt accompanying her mistaken repudiation of her mother's selflessness toward her father, who was none other than the famous Norman Cousins, with his famous illness. We can understand that a feeling of being misled by liberal feminism would spark more than a defensiveness, but an animosity toward feminism. That animosity is indeed present in Shapiro's writings but usually in the more subtle form of mockery.

Yaffa Ganz in *All Things Considered ... From a Woman's Point of View...* takes the defense of relationality one step further. Her book is an anecdotal personal narrative, making witty observations about life, nothing deep or intellectual. It certainly does not seek to answer philosophical questions about the value of woman's role in traditional Judaism. Yet, embedded within her writing is a sort of radical feminism, Orthodox style, a rousing call to religious Jewish women to appreciate their own worth and power.

The book's preface serves to remind the reader that its observations are uniquely feminine and that femininity is *more elevated than masculinity*. Despite Ganz's lighthearted style in the body of her book, this radical feminist statement in her preface infers that her book, more than a defense against feminist attacks, seeks to forge its own brand of Orthodox "feminism" based on female relationality.

> Although they are usually referred to as the "weaker sex," women possess unusual strengths. There is no lack of stories about great men, of course, but the sneaking suspicion remains: Women are the world's real Rock of Gibraltar....
>
> But women are more than just strong. They are smart and loving, sympathetic and joyful and creative. They are endowed with certain instinctive gifts whose exact definition has eluded scientific analysis to this day: The *binah yeseirah* (extra understanding) which our Sages mentioned a few thousand years ago, and the special *neshamah* which G-d crafted for them to function as the *ezer*, that indispensable partner to man.
>
> As part of their unique equipment, women have special "antennae" which run like long threads throughout human history and society, keeping them finely attuned to the needs of the people they

know and love. The information they supply helps make our world a happier, better, and more heavenly place.

Perhaps this is why the *Maharal* of Prague views women as being a higher form of creation; a creature whose innate spiritual make-up is somehow more in tune with the world of the spirit, therefore requiring the performance of fewer mitzvos than men in order to achieve spiritual perfection."[134]

In a later work, *Cinnamon and Myrrh*, Ganz's approach is mocking. In the following passage, from an essay entitled "Sarah's Daughters," we can see that Ganz accuses feminism of having deluded separatist intentions, of fighting against relationality and interdependence. She suggests that feminism has nothing to offer the Jewish woman.

> You can't write a book nowadays without mentioning Women (capital "W"). Women, you see, are in style. Once, I thought that women (small "w") were just regular people. Different from men, of course, but human beings just the same. It seems that I was wrong. Now I'm told that Women are a unique creation with their own lives to lead, their own stars to follow. No longer satisfied with being a part of the human race, they want to set up their own track and run the race alone. Their goals are 1) to stay separate from men so that 2) they can catch up with them, 3) get in front of them, and 4) be just like them, but 5) better. If you aren't sure you understand, there are Women's Studies in universities all over the world where you can learn about these things. So, not wishing to be the only contemporary writer around who writes only about women, I decided to say something about Women as well.
>
> The crucial questions are: Is the Women's Revolution good for the Jews? Is it good for Jewish women? Will it lead us towards bigger and better things? Since, after the destruction of the Temple, the gift of prophecy was given not to women (nor to men either), but only to children and fools, I dare not attempt a reply. I will only state that some of my best friends are women.[135]

Ganz asserts that women's identity must be based on her relations to men, or that search for identity becomes a farce. She mocks feminists in the primary goal she ascribes to them of staying "separate from men." Based on the above passage, we could easily label Ganz an anti-feminist; however, the previous passage, in which she overstates women's strengths, complicates this assessment. Using

Ganz's technique of capitalization, I would say that Ganz is opposed to Feminism but not feminism. She is not opposed to (at least certain aspects of) feminist theory or principles. What she does oppose is (at least certain aspects of) the political and theoretical manifestation of feminism. It is not clear to her that the political upheaval inspired by feminism ("the Women's Revolution") has been good for Jewish women. Her ambivalence toward feminism is largely founded on the liberal feminist denigration of relationality as a constructive route to self-identity.

In another personal narrative, *How Long the Night* by Mindy Gross, we see how Gross's relationship to God, like Shapiro's, expresses itself in a sanctification of the mundane, and through this relationship comes her self-development and identity. Here, the autobiographer faces the challenges of infertility, then multiple miscarriages and illness. Stylistically, she describes the challenges in her life and then switches to the mental, spiritual meanderings that help her endure the hardships. The reader feels as if she is traveling with the writer back and forth between her roles as suffering mother and spiritual fighter, from physicality to spirituality.

Gross's challenge is that she cannot (at first) become a mother. She is denied (for a while) her full female identity and must face an unwanted emptiness. She bases her selfhood on a relation to motherhood. However, this identity is painful and obscured because the relation is really a nonrelation, a nothingness. Thus, she finds it hard to be with herself.

> Instead of dwelling on the sorrow, I would flick on the light and quickly insert a tape into the stereo. Within minutes a pot would be simmering on the stove. I could not take the silent stillness very long. I always had to fill my environment, be it classroom or home, with sounds and action. In my apartment, however, the silence was not merely an unwanted guest, but a tenant I could not evict.
> Though I knew this unwelcome occupant was never completely chased away by conversation and music, I always tried my best; I put on "the tunes," changed into my cooking attire, and headed into the kitchen to start preparing dinner. I was chopping the vegetables to the rhythm.... Faster, faster ... I boiled some water.... The kitchen got hotter and more crowded.... I was beating back the cold stillness. In less than half an hour the aroma of fresh vegetable soup wafted through the rooms. I felt as if I had won — at least temporarily.[136]

Gross turns again and again to Jewish sources as she learns to face her infertility. Her longing for motherhood turns into spiritual exploration. She finds empathy in Jewish thought for her natural quest for reconciliation with hardship. She battles with the reality of her barrenness by recognizing the two planes of contention, physical and spiritual.

> The Ramban eloquently explains Rivkah's [biblical Rebecca's] perception of the world as she struggled with a difficult pregnancy. Rivkah exclaimed, as the children struggled within her, "If this is so, why am I thus?" The Ramban sees her question as a deep and heart-wrenching existential one. "Why am I in the world?" ... It is, perhaps, difficult for an outsider to identify with the depth of pain the childless woman experiences. For me, an Orthodox Jewish woman, knowing the value that our traditions have placed on having a family only accentuated the pain. Again and again I obeyed the natural womanly instinct to cry forth in woe: *Why me?*[137]

Gross, like Shapiro, believes that her self-realization (partly) opposes secular, Western culture.

> Growing up, I believed that the whole world was a smorgasbord for those who wish to partake of it. The trick lay simply in making enough of an effort. But now the effort expended made no discernible difference. My Western upbringing included in its philosophy the belief that WE can control our lives, WE have the technology to make things happen. But where in all this philosophizing was the truth that God has a few things to say about what goes on in His universe? My "control" ethic was falling apart before my eyes.[138]

Also like Shapiro, Gross's quest does not include any resistance to male consciousness. The men in her life, in this case her husband, rabbis and doctors, are not perceived as a threat to her selfhood and self-transcendence. In fact, they enter her life as she chooses and in very potent ways. She, too, finds support and solidarity with a rabbi with whom she identifies as a courageous fellow sufferer. The rabbi lost his wife and eleven children in the Nazi death camps and remained in Europe after the war to reunite families.

> I was very receptive to the healing power of the rebbe's prayers and wise words. My contact with him — a fellow "sufferer" and "survivor"

by any standards — gave me tremendous hope.... By this point in my odyssey, I had come to see the world as divided into two groups: the sufferers and the non-sufferers. The rebbe was in my camp, he was a sufferer too. I felt that he did not have to "project," to try to understand; I felt that he implicitly empathized.... I certainly felt that my struggles paled in comparison to his; if he could wake up each morning and get out of bed, then so could I.[139]

We have seen several personal narratives that demonstrate the typically feminine aspects that Mary Mason defined: "self-realization and self-transcendence through the recognition of another."[140] Another personal narrative, Ruchoma Shain's *All for the Boss*, interestingly incorporates feminine as well as masculine aspects of autobiography, which are described in the introduction to *Life/Lines: Theorizing Women's Autobiography*. Editors Bella Brodzki and Celeste Schenck tell us that the typical male autobiographer sees himself as a transcendent representation of the self, or a mirror of the universal condition. He "assumes the conflation of masculinity and humanity, canonizing the masculine representative self of both writer and reader."[141] Ruchoma Shain does not canonize the "masculine representative self," but she does posit herself as the transcendent narrator, reflecting values that are universal to the religious Jew.

Shain's writing contains none of the self-searching qualities we see in Shapiro's and Gross's writings. *All for the Boss* documents the life of an ardent, righteous man; her book is a biography of her father but also an autobiography of the early years of her life. Shain's narrative voice is transcendent, mirroring the deeds and thoughts of a man whose own spiritual quest lies beyond the realm of ordinary men, yet from whom we can derive inspiration. Her father's towering identity is not dependent on his relations with others, indeed, he transforms them.

Her transcendent narrative voice imitates that of male autobiographies, yet it is feminine in that Shain's identity is extremely dependent on her father's identity. Her story, at least in her early years, is the story of her father. Her identity is subsumed within his, yet the narrative voice is hers, transcendent and individual. We see a total collusion with, even a dependence upon, male consciousness alongside a complete acceptance of her ability as a woman to represent universal values. Shain's writing is a fusion of male and female aspects of autobiography. Her work differs mostly from Shapiro's and Gross's writings in its lack of relationality and self-searching. Why?

The answer is twofold. First, Shain is not a *baalat teshuva*. She was nurtured under the wings of a pious mother and father. She did not need the self-searching of a religious Jewish woman who was raised in an irreligious home. She did not forge a new identity for herself in adulthood. In her youth, Shain absorbed the values that she was later able to impart. She is qualified to represent the values that are universal to a religious Jewish audience. Her life growing up with an exemplary father and mother is reflected in her self-contained, self-assured narrative voice.

Second, Ruchoma Shain is the "elder statesman" among religious women writers, even though *All for the Boss* is her first book. She began a writing career at the late age of 68, when she was already a known character among religious Jewish women. Her writing reflects maturity and knowledge of the value of her role as a woman in the Jewish community, as well as the self-confidence to go beyond the bounds of gender role playing. She is a personality, a teacher of her society's values to both women and men, beyond being just a writer.

Shain's narrative voice is an exception to the voice we usually hear in the ultra–Orthodox women's narratives, which is confessional, personal, painful and relational. She speaks from a position of maturity, from a position of one whose center (traditional Judaism) has always been stable in her consciousness. Her frame of mind is prefeminist, transcending feminism. The voices of *baalot teshuva* we hear in most of the personal narratives are feeling their way over to ultra–Orthodox Judaism from feminism. Their center is shifting. Their frame of mind is younger, more postmodern in that the positing of their "I" is completely contextual and individual. We will again hear the transcendent narrative voice, which we heard in Shain's book, when we look at the Holocaust testimonials, which were also written by mature, prefeminist women from ultra–Orthodox backgrounds.

CHAPTER SEVEN

Anthologies:
"Secret Struggles"

The growing popularity of anthologies is a fairly recent development in ultra–Orthodox literature written in the English language.
While the contributing writers are male and female in some of the
anthologies, with women writers as the clear majority, some anthologies are exclusively women's writings. Most of the anthologies are made
up of personal narratives, though they may contain some fiction. There
is one anthology that contains only fiction.

Most of the anthologies have been edited by a select (female) few,
giving a uniformity of tone and message to the collections. The issues
that Sarah Shapiro enumerated in *Growing with My Children* appear
in the pages of these anthologies; indeed, she has edited most of them.
The issues are familiar: holiness versus the commonplace, identity,
resisting feminism with Torah ideals, incorporating feminism into
Torah ideals — in short, the place of the ultra–Orthodox Jewish woman
in contemporary society.

It is difficult to define the overall literary voice in these anthologies, but Yaffa Ganz in *Cinnamon and Myrrh* describes it well in her
discussion of modern Jewish women:

> Today's women are probably the most cosmopolitan, most versatile,
> best educated, and most confused generation of Jewish women the
> world has ever seen. They are engaged in complex, multiple activi-
> ties while searching for a single, definitive, clear-cut identity and
> role. When you think of it, it definitely is confusing.[142]

The literary voice in the ultra–Orthodox anthologies may not be
"confusing," but it is eclectic, a formulation of the struggle of women

grappling with conflicting ideas about their role. The search is for a clarity of identity, and it is typically the search of the *baalat teshuva*, the woman entering the fold of Orthodoxy from a secular upbringing. But the struggle is not hers alone.

Of Home and Heart: Reflections on the World of the Jewish Woman opens with an introduction by Sarah Shapiro, the book's editor, which sets the tone for the anthology and gives us an agenda of concerns.

> It gradually became apparent that there was a force within me, an irrepressible drive toward something or other, and that there was no way it could be squashed.... I simply *was*, eternally, a Jewish mother. But what was it about me that made it so?...
>
> All I knew is that whatever it was I feared, I was missing the point if I defined it in terms of the easy targets of America's derisive mirth. It was, in truth, something that at its roots was intrinsic to my nature, my Jewish nature, something that the comedians and literati had deprecated because they, too, were scared. And a receptive audience across the land had chimed in, in order to distance themselves from this concealed principle of our culture:
>
> *Beware: What an unappreciated fool you'll be, if you give so much you give yourself away.*[143]

Giving, credited as a Jewish and intrinsically feminine ideal, becomes the essence of the conflict of the contemporary religious Jewish woman: giving, yet not losing the self in the process, either by giving too much or by denying the giving nature of the self. After much soul-searching and a talk with *Rebbetzin* Tziporah Heller, renowned women's educator and author of *More Precious than Pearls,* Shapiro comes to the conclusion that only the woman who is spiritually full can truly give — and included in spiritual fullness are women's status and ego needs, intellectual needs and real spiritual needs. The whole anthology, then, is a discussion and debate of the spiritual fulfillment of the Jewish woman — her growth, even amidst adversity — for the sake of giving.

In Bracha Druss Goetz's poem "Between the Braids," the poet must resist the adversity of demanding people and foreign ideas, as well as the adversity of mundane drudgery. Listen to the poet's "secret struggles" not to lose the self in the process of giving — and also not to forget the holiness in "simple giving":

What's in the spaces between the braids
Of these new *challahs*[144] I just made?
How much of me is hidden there?
Between the braids, my thoughts appear.

First I sifted the flour through
Thinking of what else I could do.
Who wants to be here baking bread?
I could write my first book instead.

I added each ingredient
And wondered why my soul was sent.
I cracked two eggs and then two more.
Is this what I was created for?

"*Shabbos Kodesh, Shabbos Kodesh*,"[145] my lips whisper,
hands knead the dough.
Let me see my work is holy. Raising high
what seems so low.

Does the *challah* absorb frustration?
Does the *challah* hear my voice so shrill?
Does the *challah* absorb my confusion?
As it rises on the window sill?...

Stuck here in the kitchen and still longing for fame.
When did simple giving get such a bad name?

"*Shabbos Kodesh, Shabbos Kodesh*" — Open up my eyes.
Let me see my work is holy. Let me stop chasing lies....

When every crumb has vanished from the *challahs*
    that I made
What will remain? Just my secret struggles. Offered up
    between the braids.[146]

The tension, the "secret struggle," of finding an integrated identity as an observant Jewish woman is universal to the voice of the *baalot teshuva*. Yet it is an intrinsically ironic feature because these women have *chosen* to take up this struggle. The *baalat teshuva* has chosen the lifestyle of ultra–Orthodox women even though it entails contradictions for her. There is a contradiction between what she feels and what she knows, or between what she feels and what she would like to feel. Her upbringing in a society suffused with feminist consciousness has her doubting the holiness inherent in menial things, which "seem so low," such as baking bread for the Sabbath. This is what she *feels*, but what she *knows* is that her "work is holy." She admits a painful problem: She cannot "open up [her] eyes." She knows that her heart chases lies, but it seems to have a will of its own. She *feels* that she is "stuck" in the kitchen, but she *knows* that with divine assistance, she will see the real holiness of her work.

The struggle of the *baalat teshuva* is integrating secular, Western, feminist values into those of traditional Judaism. Judaism, as her absolute value system, cannot always accommodate the values that were assimilated into her psyche in the past.[147] Baking *challah*, Sabbath bread, is indicative of this struggle. Baking bread is an optional activity, not a commandment, but it is a way of enhancing the Sabbath atmosphere. The *baalat teshuva* in the poem is engaged in an activity that is not required of her but one that she knows from experience will enhance the Sabbath spirit in her home. We see her exercising her religious prerogatives: She chooses to bake bread to make her Sabbath table more delectable, more special. She wants the emotional satisfaction involved in devoting herself, giving of herself completely to fulfilling every aspect of traditional life, including baking the bread for her Sabbath table. The problem is that the practical details of what this means in her life, i.e., sifting flour, cracking eggs, kneading dough, in short, being "stuck" in the kitchen, has been given a "bad name" by her own sensibilities, sensibilities that were shaped by a Western feminist consciousness. So, she needs help. She doesn't feel that her work is holy, even though she knows it must be. Her belief in the whole framework of traditional Judaism impels her to continue the actions even though her heart has not caught up with her head, so to speak. She experiences a dissonance between how she thinks and how she feels and recognizes that outwardly she plays the part, but inwardly she still "chas[es] lies."

In Goetz's poem "Wonder Woman," we hear the struggle between giving and remaking one's identity, the struggle of choosing what she should give herself to and how and in what mold she should remake herself. Through the metaphor of her puppet show, she grapples with the question of which show she wants to perform in, that is, in which role she chooses to play out her life. She also grapples with the question of which life role is real and which is a "show," which role is a temporary, unsatisfying "show" and which is lasting and meaningful. Listen to the struggle of the *baalat teshuva* who seeks not only to forge a new path in her life but to refashion the way she thinks ("If I could only realize…"). Metaphorically, this is to "unweave" the old "tapestries." Her greatest struggle lies in her own unfulfilled determination to change her mental construct:

> I worked so hard just to make them all so proud
> Pre-med grind — way back to spelling tests.
> I worked hard just to make them all so proud.
> Then they'd know — it would *show* — I was best.
> So why'd it always happen I could not convince myself?
> Awards just made a hollow sound when placed upon the shelf.
> And why'd it always happen that the praises stopped so fast?
> Isn't there a goal to reach where my glory will last?
>
> Then one day I got tired of this game.
> Wonder girl, though you've won, what's it worth?
> Then one day I got tired of this game.
> Craving more, is it found here on earth?
> Well it has not been easy putting old wishes aside.
> While washing piles of dishes, my hands burn with swallowed pride.
> No, it has not been easy putting old wishes aside.
> Though I'm called mother now, the old dreams never died.
>
> .   .   .   .
>
> Their eyes were full of wonder as they watched my puppet show.
> My whole life I've been waiting for applause.
> Well it came — and it's true — it was great.
> My whole life I've waited for *this* applause.
> Their little hands — clapping for joy — were worth the wait
> If I could only realize that here within these walls
> I did something much greater than in all the lecture halls.
> If I could only realize that this glory does not leave —
> Why are elusive tapestries the hardest to unweave?[148]

Again and again we hear the voice of the *baalat teshuva* consistently seeking to repossess her individual, unencumbered consciousness, to sever it from the consciousness she discovers within herself at some point in her religious maturity and with which she is not satisfied. She seeks to dissociate from certain values, which were part of her induction into Western culture and which she feels are negative.

Tangible Metaphors, Intangible Quest

The anthologies *Our Lives* and *More of Our Lives* are repositories of the ultra–Orthodox woman's issues we have discussed: her forging of identity through relationality, the conflict inherent in giving, the duality of her position as a divine and a mundane being and the constant quest for self-transcendence that duality implies.

As readers, we feel the author's desire to speak to us, to make contact. She wants to get to the bottom of things, to tell us what her life is about, which is what our lives are about. Alicia Ostriker finds this pattern in contemporary American women's poetry, and it is relevant for us to note that she associates it with the raw physical images we see in that poetry.

> I believe that it is the contact imperative which finally accounts for the confessional or diarist mode in women's writing, because of the intimacy this mode imposes on the audience.... As the poet refuses to distance herself from her emotions, so she prevents us from distancing ourselves. We are obliged to witness, to experience the hot breath of the poem upon us. Or perhaps we want to wrestle loose. The poem is impolite, crude, it imposes too much. In either case, we have been obliged to some degree to relinquish our roles as readers, and to respond personally.[149]

In American women's poetry, the "hot breath" of the poem may be sex, violence, birth, death, bloodshed, perversion or any combination thereof. Physicality is shocking and imposing upon the reader, as Ostriker demonstrates. Since we are "obliged to witness," the poetry coerces the reader into a voyeuristic engagement. However, the physicality in ultra–Orthodox writing, through which the author exposes or, more correctly, shares herself with the reader is never crude. Physical and earthy, yes, but not shocking or imposing. There is a strong "contact imperative" between writer and reader, and while physicality is a mode and a means, it is not an end, not an expression of identity as we find in American women's poetry. Ultra-Orthodox women writers do not utilize the metaphor of the woman's body. It is too personal, too immodest, and its exposure hazards its defilement. The metaphors of physicality that *are* used do not represent her concrete identity but rather her spiritual identity. The language of physicality is the means. It is the way women speak, the way they understand each other. Harsh metaphors do not serve the religious Jewish woman's purpose.

The symbol of physicality in Bracha Druss Goetz's poem "Between the Braids" is bread. Bread is enough. A more shocking metaphor is not used in place of this universal symbol of physicality in every woman's life. The ultra–Orthodox reader understands that the poet is sharing with us her conflict between physical and ethereal demands. Baking bread is a woman's metaphor, the language she uses so that other women will relate to her. Since the metaphor is incidental to the spiritual struggle she is revealing, it is also transient. In Varda Branfman's poem "Bread," bread is not physicality but spirituality. Through tangible metaphors, the poet describes her internal, intangible quest.

Everywhere I am looking for bread.

In the middle of a conversation,
I am uneasy.
I open my fist to see
if there is a crust of bread.

Nothing, not even a crumb.
I can't go on, I'm so hungry.

When I sit on the bus
I look down at my feet
and across the aisle.
There are mouths moving
and I wonder:
"Do they have bread?"
This question haunts me
wherever I go:
"Is each step bringing me closer
or farther away?"

Today I passed a tiny woman,
bent and old,

who very slowly closed
a gate behind her.
She picked up her head
and smelled the air.
She knows about bread.
I kept moving down the street
with my hunger.

You ask me what I want
in a husband —
I want bread.

When everyone goes indoors
in the heat of the day
and sleeps,
the bread bakes.

There are people whose sleep is bread,
but not for me.

In my father's house
we ate bread.

When he spoke
his eyes were innocent and happy.

My father's death was bread again
but I ran away.

Now I know about bread.
I can't live without it.
When I put my head to the stones of the Wall
it is bread.[150]

The "Wall" is the Western Wall in Jerusalem, where Jewish lore says that the divine presence is always found. The divine presence is the poet's bread. Only this "bread" satisfies her hunger. The poem extends the biblical metaphor in Amos 8:11, "Behold, days are coming, says the Lord God, when I will send a famine in the land; not a famine for bread, nor a thirst for water, but for hearing the words of God."

Food and hunger represent spiritual yearning. Goetz's poems

express the yearning to transcend the physicality that traps her. Branf-man's yearning for spirituality *is* (metaphorically) a hunger for the physical, for bread. The common ground for both of these religious women poets and many others is that the physical world embodies holiness, which we may not see or find. The true yearning, and the goal of self-revelation, is to grasp for herself and enable the reader to grasp the intangibility of the tangible. The metaphor of physicality is more true than not. In the end, the yearning *is* for the physical, for real life, not for its own sake but for the godliness inherent within it.[151]

Sarah Shapiro expresses Ostriker's "contact imperative," ultra–Orthodox style, in her introduction to *More of Our Lives*, which is entitled "Reading and Writing as I Openers."

> Why did G-d create the human desire for stories? I can't presume to know, but I can guess: He didn't want us to be limited by our physical selves. Where our thoughts are, that's where we are. We're figments of our own imaginations. Only we of all G-d's creations have hunger of the mind, a hunger that can be fed with words.
>
> Once upon a time there was a woman (you). She lived in a house and swept the floor and put away the clothes, then sat down with a book and began to read. The story went like this:
>
> I'm alone. I want to be surrounded.
>
> I'm surrounded. I want to be by myself.
>
> I don't want to be just me. I want a multiplicity of viewpoints. I want peepholes into other people's lives. I can't just stop them on the sidewalk and ask.
>
> I'm assailed by the world. I need a refuge.
>
> I'm trapped by the house. I need a doorway.
>
> I'm full, my cup runneth over. Each moment, if I respond to it, can answer my deepest needs.
>
> I'm hungry. The world passes by so fast, I want to take a longer look. I want the world. I want to hold it in my hands.
>
> Give me a book.[152]

She concludes, "What hunger is it that a story can quell? The hunger for our own lives."[153]

Shapiro conflates the allegorization of spirituality *and* literary expression with the physical metaphor of hunger. She then decon-structs the metaphor by telling us that it is not a metaphor at all, or not completely, but the real search for a meaningful physicality, which is a combination of the spiritual and the physical, soul and body: "our own lives." And, as the title of her introduction implies, in the spiritual yearning for an artistic expression of "our own lives," we discover who we are.

Memory and Mother

In ultra–Orthodox women's personal narratives, especially those of *baalot teshuva*, we see an almost mystical connection between memory and the image of the mother.[154] This phenomenon is readily apparent in the anthologies because one sees many short writings grouped together. Even a look at a single anthology reveals how pervasive the mother's presence in memory is. As the ultra–Orthodox writer looks into her past, those moments that are deemed pivotal are often associated with her mother, her relationship with her mother, her memory of her mother or herself as mother.

It is not surprising that recollections of the mother preoccupy the *baalat teshuva*, who by definition is concerned with "returning" to her national/religious roots. In her quest to carve out a new role for herself that incorporates traditional Judaism, she explores female Jewish models and her own past. The mother occupies a space in both, in personal memory and as an accessible model. The writer does mental housecleaning, discerning which of the values she currently holds — which were originally demonstrated in her society and, very likely, in her mother — should be consciously reabsorbed and which eschewed. Thus, we see her either identifying with her mother and the example of Jewish femininity she embodies, or dissociating from her and the values she represents.

But the mother focus goes beyond its placement in the writers' problem of identity integration to an elusive connection with the collective Jewish past and future. The writer views the mother (her own mother and herself as mother) as a link in the chain of Jewish continuity. She is not just a woman who has a daughter or the daughter of a woman; rather, she occupies a particular niche in the mysterious process of Jewish survival. Each child born, though he may be one of many,[155] or each child lost, though there are already six children in the family,[156] is respectively fortunate or tragic in both a micro- and macrocosmic way. The mother rejoices or mourns as an individual mother and as a mother raising a child of her people, yet one more link in the continuity of its traditions. She is doubly vulnerable to the fate of her children, which contributes to our understanding of the preoccupation with the memory of the mother.

The mother's voice from the past can sometimes have an ethereal, mysterious effect. For example, "Miriam bas Leiba" publishes a letter that she has translated from the original Yiddish. It was written by a mother to her little girl of two years. We discover that the mother sewed the letter into her little girl's undershirt before sending her off to safety in a child rescue during the Holocaust. The mother expects her own death in the near future, and she wanted her child to know that she had parents who loved her and to have testimony that this war was not just another war: "that all the wars in the world don't add up to the agony in my heart right now as I write this."[157] Miraculously, the letter did stay with the child. After reading the letter, we are informed that "Miriam bas Leiba," the writer, is that child, who decided to publish her mother's letter anonymously nearly 50 years later in order to teach other mothers, women today, how much they should appreciate having and holding their children. Her (mother's?) lesson, a voice from the tragic past, reverberates heavily.

Another voice from the past is Gillah Amoch, whose letters to her mother were published after her and her sister's tragic deaths in a car accident. We hear the faith, youth and hopefulness of a 20-year-old girl studying in a college for *baalot teshuva*.[158] And then the next article in the anthology is by Gillah's mother, the voice of pain and confusion: "I stare into the sifting whiteness and see Time as a long, straight line without beginning, without end.... Our capacity for understanding in this world is too limited.... I cannot absorb the shock, reality shudders against the walls erected in my mind. No amount of screaming or appealing will help. I am confused."[159] The juxtaposition of these two articles creates an anguished, surreal couplet. The one, bursting with youth, life and love for her mother; the other, written after her daughters' deaths, also full of love but containing pain and loss, too. Two women, mother and daughter, who can only meet through their writing, placed side by side between the covers of a religious women's anthology.

Joanne Jackson Yelenik describes how growing up the daughter of "greenhorns," immigrants from Eastern Europe, made her supersensitive to the fact that she was not as "American as [her] girlfriends."[160] She spent many years distancing herself from the image attached to Jewish women, including her own mother, who were lauded as *balabustas*, devoted homemakers whose pride and joy were cooking and cleaning. Yelenik writes:

> As soon as I heard the word, with all the glowing homemaking quali-
> ties and hearth-like values it conveyed, I knew I hated it. Hated the
> word, the idea and the association I had with it: Endless platters of
> heavy, greasy food, thick-iced cakes, aprons and a never-ending stream
> of relatives — eating, laughing, talking, reminiscing about the Old
> Country, teasing Cousin Charlie about his *Galicianer* connections.[161]

Her article is full of irony and humor. As much as she tries to detach herself from the Jewish mother's image she perceives, she cannot help but marvel at her mother's ability and devotion. As much as she finds the *balabusta* "dangerous" to her self-image, Yelenik discovers that her qualities are largely a part of her own nature. When she becomes removed from the threat of the *balabusta*— when Brooklyn becomes her "Old Country"— then past threats to her identity become fond reminiscences about a lost world. Only then is she able to view the *balabusta*— and herself as one of them — with pride.

Then there are those writers who speak of their mothers as if they were wizards performing magical feats in some far-off domain, incredible and inimitable. Chana Siegel's mother's domain was her sewing room, where she whipped out women's fashions with the speed and precision of an enchanted couturiere. Siegel feels that talent of her mother's caliber is rare and inimitable, comparable to the accomplishments of the great masters: "She herself rarely halted in mid-garment except for a cup of coffee. I've often thought that's what DaVinci must have been like while painting the Mona Lisa."[162] Chaya Rivkah Jessel speaks of her mother's magical domain, the balcony garden, as a "wondrous array of plant life" so well "nurtured and luscious."[163]

Both of these writers recollect their mothers' accomplishments because they epitomize important lessons, which their mothers as role models gave them. Memories of their mothers are important insofar as they represent values that these writers carry through life. Siegel gleaned from her mother's example how to "strive for good value."[164] And Jessel writes that if her mother noticed a particular plant not thriving, she would, if necessary, rearrange her whole balcony in order to ensure it received the required amount of heat/wind/sunlight/shade. By way of this example, my mother sowed the seeds for *my* eventual transplantation — giving me the courage to uproot my whole life in order to enhance my spiritual survival.[165]

Jessel largely credits her mother with her eventual religiosity. She claims that her mother's example planted the seed that blossomed into her transformation, a transformation ironically, that seems on the surface to go against her mother, who was not Orthodox. Debra Renee Kaufman, in her sociological study on *baalot teshuva, Rachel's Daughters: Newly Orthodox Jewish Women*, found that many women who become religiously observant attribute their decisions to their mothers. They claim that the essential values that were stressed in the home were those they saw manifested in Orthodox Jewish life. And the women Kaufman interviewed made such claims even though their families were vehemently opposed to their becoming religious. So even as the *baalot teshuva* move away from their secular upbringings, they believe that they are true to the essential parental message they received in the home, true to the memory of their parents.

Sarah Shapiro even had the rare privilege of hearing her father, Norman Cousins, tell her shortly before his death that he was glad she led a religious life. Shapiro was astonished because they "had been carrying on a twenty-year dialogue about the religion" with neither side yielding. However, he had obviously concluded that her observant lifestyle was "consistent with [his] values."[166]

CHAPTER EIGHT

Holocaust Testimonials

Holocaust testimonials are a completely different type of personal narrative than the ones we have already looked at. Female and male survivors of the Holocaust have undertaken to share their experiences with religious readers. These testimonials are written by survivors who emerged from the Holocaust horrors with their faith intact, remaining practicing Jews. Why did they write their stories? What do they want us to hear?

The following is a statement by CIS Publishers about their Holocaust series: "*The Holocaust Diaries* is a collection of distinguished memoirs of survivors whose rocklike faith was tested in the fiercest crucible in history, true heroes who emerged stronger than before and rebuilt a new Jewish world on the ashes of the old." Each and every story is a testimonial to the faith of these survivors. They are courageous, and they are strong, but their most outstanding achievement from a traditional Jewish perspective is that they did not lose their faith in God.

In Pearl Benisch's preface to her book *To Vanquish the Dragon,* we hear her "rocklike" faith, which impelled her to write her story. We also hear the extreme affirmative power of her voice, a tone that runs throughout all the ultra–Orthodox women's Holocaust narratives, a tone almost too positive and strong to believe. They sound as if they never broke, never succumbed to doubt. Could these ultra–Orthodox women survivors have soared so high above the flames of genocide that their faith in the God of their people was never singed?

> The great Rabbis, the leaders, the wise and the smart and the simple, the rich and the poor, they went all together. Why were we singled out to survive when they all were condemned to die? I do not know. Such was the Will of God.

> But one thing I do know. If we were saved, it was for a purpose:
> to continue the chain of Jewish heritage and to tell and retell to the
> next generations the story of our People.
>
> How they had lived in those trying times and how they had died.
> To vividly recall their struggles and to acclaim their triumphs.
> To tell our youth about the conquest of human dignity over the
> bestiality of man.
> To show how man can plunge into the deepest pit of evil and
> become worse than a beast.
> And to demonstrate the greatness of human beings who can soar
> to the loftiest heights and become greater than angels.
> These righteous ones taught us what no book will ever teach us:
> the meaning of faith and trust in God. The meaning of *tzedaka*
> [charity] and *gemilas chesed* [loving kindness].
> Let all generations to come know the truth: that no nation stood
> up for our rights, no country — not even the one that proudly pro-
> claims: "Give us your tired, your poor, your huddled masses..." —
> opened its doors to save the oppressed Jews. We have only one
> friend, one ally to Whom we can turn in despair. Only Hashem
> [God] is our Savior and He promised us that *"Am Yisrael Chai"* —
> the nation of Israel lives — and that He will rescue us and redeem
> us.[167]

Many religious Jews who went through the Holocaust did not
remain practicing Jews. Until recently, the prevalent perspective about
the Holocaust has been one in which the Jews are seen as helpless victims for not fighting back against the Nazis, for going "like sheep to
the slaughter."[168] Religious Holocaust testimonials defy this. In the
strict sense of the word, the Jewish people *were* the victims of the
Holocaust, of course. Yet the stories of those who survived not only
in body but also in spirit prove that victimization is largely a state of
mind. The Holocaust testimonials demonstrate that, while the body
may be victimized, the spirit remains free. These stories share with
us the lives of women and men who not only fought to preserve every
last ounce of human dignity but who also fought to remain faithful
to traditional Judaism. These survivors' accounts challenge old perspectives by showing us that heroism is not only to be found in mil-
itarism, such as the Warsaw Ghetto uprising.

> "You," he said hoarsely, "my dear, dear children." It was a tremen-
> dous effort for him to talk to us in such a civil manner. "You are

going ... home now. The war is over. You are free." He seemed to choke over the word. "You have a future." With shaking hands he ripped off all the medals glittering on his uniform and threw them on the ground. The proud, arrogant Hauptmann stood before us, humble and crushed. "You have a future, but as for me, I don't know." He started to cry as he turned away from us and began to walk to his car.

No one moved. Five hundred girls just stood there and let a murderer walk away. All of the SS officers had disappeared during Hauptmann's speech; there were no guards, no guns trained on us, nothing to stop us from pouncing on that hated man and ripping him to shreds. Yet we stood there and watched him walk away. Something held us back from sinking to that final level of murder. Perhaps it was our final act of defiance. We showed that Nazi that, unlike the Germans, a Jew always behaves like a human being, no matter what the circumstances.[169]

Holocaust critics have not always been sensitive in their interpretations of Jewish reactions to Nazi oppression. This excerpt demonstrates how Holocaust history is incomplete without the victims' testimony; hearing the victims' voices can give us a different perspective on history. The inaction of the women in the above excerpt may be interpreted as complacency and weakness, but the author clearly expresses her opinion that it was dignity, defiance and strength that shaped their silent consensus not to react. Hearing the author's voice, we can read their inaction as deliberate, passive activism.

Ultra-Orthodox women's narratives do not only demonstrate a universal heroic defiance but a heroism that is uniquely Jewish.

"Good Shabbos, girls," Tzila called as she approached, her unique, soft smile spread across that bright face. "Good Shabbos," she repeated, those two words reflecting all her joy upon seeing us alive.

"Good Shabbos." How do those two words sound in front of a towering chimney belching fire and clouds of black smoke? How do they sound when said amidst the stench of burning human flesh?

But it was Shabbos in the whole world, including this living inferno. Even here, God, it was Your holy Shabbos, and Your children remembered it in the authentic "*shamor v'zachor*" way. The candles Tzila lit every Friday eve dispelled the darkness of the night and reminded the inmates that Shabbos had come to Birkenau.[170] Even in this hell they kept Your commandments as much as possible, regardless of the sacrifice involved. "Good Shabbos," Tzila said.

But what, I wondered, was so good about Shabbos here? One glance at Tzila's face told me. It's good to see you alive. It's good to be alive, even inside this sack of skin and bones. It's good to stay human in this bestial world. It remains "Good Shabbos" as long as one feels hope and faith and the Divine spark inside.[171]

These stories demonstrate the heroism of the spirit. They are full of eyewitness accounts of spiritual heroism, example after example of a determination to make human dignity the highest priority in the face of utter degradation and death, a determination to never let moral freedom be crushed. These survivors tell us that the heroism of their people lies in the moral and spiritual imperative to sacrifice their individual lives for the sake of others.

I'll never forget the time when I saw Kayla risk her life to get a little soup. We were all standing in line outside the blocks to receive our meager portions of soup. The *kapos* and *blokowas* were walking up and down the line, slapping their truncheons against their palms for emphasis. Vicious dogs strained against their leashes, eager to pounce on a helpless Jew when given the command. Suddenly, I saw Kayla darting up the road toward the kettles of soup. It took her only a second or two to dip a small pot into one of the kettles and hurry back into line. I stared at her, open-mouthed. How did she do that? How could she risk it? How did she manage to get away with it without getting caught?...

"Kayla!" I said with a little gasp. "I-I don't believe it! What made you do that? Why did you —"

It was Aunt Bluma who replied. "Kayla has arranged food for me before," she said. "What bothers me the most is that after all that, you would think she would at least taste a little bit of the soup that she gets for me. But she makes me drink every last drop."[172]

Religious Holocaust testimonials tell us that camp inmates not only risked their lives for other people but also for a single Torah precept. Fulfilling religious commandments was an act of defiance, a survival tactic, as well as a statement of physical and spiritual identity.

Men risked their lives day after day for the chance to do a single *mitzvah* [precept of Jewish law]. The most audacious schemes were carried out often with a large amount of success. It wasn't only the *frum* [religious] people, however; even those that had been non-religious joined the lines of men waiting for a chance to wear *tefillin* [phylacteries]. A *mitzvah* was something tangible to cling to in the midst of all the horrors and despair.

There was a young man named Hershel Protzel who broke his foot in the coal mines. His friends, frantic in their efforts to save him from the selections, tried hiding him in the barracks and covering for him at work, fulfilling his quota as well as their own. When they saw that he was not getting any better, they managed to pull enough strings to get him a job as latrine commando. His task was to keep the lines of people waiting for the latrine in order by issuing numbers and keeping track. He was able to do his job and stay off his broken foot without any difficulty.

Hershel took advantage of the situation. He managed to get a pair of *tefillin*. He hid the smuggled treasure in a hole in the roof of a shed, right next to the latrines. Suddenly, Hershel's latrine became the most popular one in that section of Auschwitz. Men waited impatiently in line for the chance to savor a moment of *tefillah* [prayer] while wearing *tefillin*.

Hershel, who managed to survive the death marches on his broken foot, always maintained that it was the *zchus* [merit] of *tefillin* that kept him alive.[173]

In this quote, a female survivor talks about the experience of men. But how many of these women's narratives talk about women, about the experiences that are unique to women *because* of their gender?

Joan Ringelheim, a pioneering researcher, explores aspects of the Holocaust horrors that were specific to women. She discusses the aspects of women's victimization in the camps that until recently have been largely ignored by Holocaust historians, including sexual exploitation by Nazi, gentile and Jewish men. The questions she asks and explores are controversial. Gender concerns about the Holocaust may seem irrelevant and irreverent in light of the more fundamental issue of the struggle to survive, and Ringelheim discusses her first-hand experiences with the denial of gender concerns by Holocaust scholars, including herself.[174] She and other researchers/critics of the Holocaust claim that much more needs to be researched and told about women in the Holocaust.

The testimonials of women make up a significant quantity of ultra–Orthodox Holocaust narratives, but critics complain that such is not the case with general Holocaust narratives.[175] However, there is relatively little in the religious women's narratives that is gender specific. Most likely, social propriety and modesty inhibit the retelling of sexually explicit victimization, which we readily find in general women's Holocaust narratives.[176] Yet it does not appear that religious women survivors consciously ignore or neutralize their experience and knowledge of sexual exploitation in the camps and elsewhere. It seems that these women prioritize different concerns: Their victimization as women is less important to them than their victimization as Jews. Or, perhaps, this very sexlessness is a sign of the authenticity of the writers' accounts. Holocaust scholar Alvin H. Rosenfeld writes that Holocaust testimonials prove that hunger rated as the predominant "passion," with all others, including sexuality, being "held in abeyance. As a result, one of the characteristics of Holocaust writings at their most authentic is that they are peculiarly and predominantly sexless."[177] This theory may help us understand the absence of personal sexuality in the ultra–Orthodox women's testimonials. But it still does not explain why the witnessing of sexual or sexually related victimization against women appears in general women's testimonials but is so obviously absent from ultra–Orthodox testimonials.

It is significant that most of the survivors/authors were single young women during World War II. From their stories we see that they did not normally face gender-specific victimization caused by pregnancy, childbirth, separation from children or the endangering of adults by children. There are exceptions, however. Additionally, rape does not appear as a threat or an issue of concern as it does in some general women's narratives.

In the following passage, the author, Pearl Benisch, tells the tragic story of one group of Jews who tried and failed to protect a mother and her child. She places herself as a member of the group of Jews who lived through the incident, and she speaks as one part of the "massive body of compressed human flesh." Her heart merges with its "unified heart." Yet, submerged in this story is another one, the story of the Jewish woman who is victimized *because* she is a mother protecting her child. Benisch clearly feels a stronger association with her victimized people as a whole than with the victimized mother. The larger victimization of Jewry is at least as tragic for her as the victimization of a single Jewish woman. We feel Benisch's helplessness and anger as she relives the nightmare.

Boxcars were waiting. Our turn came: we were pushed inside as tightly as possible, up to 120 human beings per car; then the two large doors were shut. We heard the clatter of a heavy padlock being clamped on....

Suddenly the doors were pried open and a sunbeam penetrated the car, bringing a little ray of hope — how we appreciated it now! In a split-second it was gone, and in its place, framed by the open doors, stood the Butcher of Plashow, the cultured savage, Amon Goeth. His face was typically Germanic, right down to its hateful look. His frigid eyes exuded spite. His huge frame blocked almost all of the sun that had tried to penetrate and cheer us up.

"Where is the child?" he shouted. "Mother and child out! *Raus!*" he roared, more venom than words. The mass of human bodies was paralyzed with fright.

"I saw a child go into the car. Where is it?" he demanded angrily.

Nobody moved. Over one hundred pairs of terrified eyes turned toward the monster. No sound was uttered, but one could hear a hundred hearts pounding in terror.

"Where is that child? If it does not come out at once, I will shoot you all, one by one!" he spat. "Give me that child!"

"There is no child here," someone dared to reply.

"I saw a child go in," Goeth shouted. "You Jewish swine, liars, smugglers. You smuggled in a child!" he howled with fury. "I will shoot you all, all!"

In this matter, we knew, he was a man of his word. Most of the people in our boxcar came from Plashow and had had the "privilege" of watching Goeth at work at his collective punishments.

As if to confirm our thoughts, he barked, "This is not an idle threat."

I shuddered, looked around, waited in tragic anticipation, and hoped against hope for a miracle....

"Give me that child!" the beast roared. From the corner of my eye I watched the mother. She squirmed as if to step forward, but her friends restrained her. A hunted animal, cornered, chosen as prey, she clutched her child under her greatcoat, sheltered the boy with her body, and prayed for a miracle.

As I observed the strained but determined faces, I knew that the human mass, with its enormous loving heart, had made up its mind.

"You idiots!" Goeth ranted. "I will blow up the car with all of you in it. Out with the child!" The human mass did not move. Its one heart pounded with determination.

But the devil, too, was determined. Since his Prussian pride would not permit him to bend to enter the boxcar, he stood on the steps and ordered his two subordinates, "Into the car and get me that child, fast!"

They pounced on us with rifle butts, truncheons, and jackboots: "All to the right!" they barked, compressing us more severely than before in order to leave some room on the left. Then they moved among us, shoving each one to the left with a kick in the behind. The maniac at the door scrutinized each moving shadow. The lackeys' truncheons came down on the bent bodies, to rush them on and finish the *Aktion*. The crowd on the left grew as that on the right, still trying to shield mother and son, decreased....

"We got her!" he yelled, his fat, red face beaming with pride. "We got them, Herr Hauptscharfuhrer, the mother and the child." Proudly he turned them over to his boss....

The door slammed shut; again we were plunged into darkness. No one spoke. The stillness was frightening, as before a thunderstorm. Then came the inevitable. Two shots pierced the air: one for the "smuggler," the other for the eleven-year-old "contraband."

The massive body of compressed human flesh, its unified heart pulsing with love, felt the pain of helplessness, of despair and disappointment. It had offered its one hundred lives on the altar of human love and sacrifice, but could not even save one Jewish child.

Yet even now, as I witnessed the triumph of evil, I felt proud to be part of this wretched, tortured, haunted, yet great people.[178]

One of the exceptions to the usually non–gender-specific testimonials of ultra–Orthodox women is R.L. Klein's account of her childbirth during the war. A young married woman when the war began, we see that she encountered dangers that an unmarried religious woman typically would not have had to face.

In 1944, she was admitted to a hospital in Budapest to give birth. The nurse refused to let Klein's husband stay near her. Close to giving birth, in heavy labor, the nurse informed her, perhaps falsely, that her baby's heartbeat had stopped: "It's as good as dead and so are you! And I don't intend to call your doctor until I'm sure that it's too late to save either one of you. Ha, Jew! ... you might as well enjoy your rest in bed, because it will be your last!"[179] Ignoring the incredible pain, she climbed out of the bed when the nurse had gone and ran to her husband outside, telling him to immediately call the doctor before it was too late. The doctor arrived shortly, and Klein and her baby girl pulled through.

Later she describes holding her baby whenever possible. She would take the baby out of her crib even when she was quiet and place her in her own bed. The future of her baby and her fear of separation provided a constant source of anxiety. Klein feels that others, including her husband, could not fathom the depths of her fears as a mother. Sure that their fake Aryan identities are about to be disclosed to the SS, Klein writes a hasty note to a gentile mother who shares her apartment building. She addresses the note to Ersabet, who she is sure is a Nazi sympathizer, and intends to hang it on the baby's bassinet when the SS comes for them. The note pleads with Ersabet to raise the child as her own, to overcome her anti–Semitism in the name of compassionate motherhood: "*I am aware of how passionately you hate Jews, but please, hear my cry. Please, please save our baby. You must understand, this is not between Gentiles and Jews. This is between two mothers' hearts.*"[180]

In a profoundly poignant scene, Ersabet and Klein, alias Zsuzsi, discover one another's true identities. During the last days of the Russian siege that liberated Budapest, these two women find themselves in the building's bomb shelter during a frightening air raid.

From time to time, my gaze fell upon Ersabet, who sat there, her face distorted with fright, rapidly telling her rosary beads and crossing her chest from time to time.

Then it happened. The house took a direct hit.

I heard the awesome sound of crumbling bricks, and with it crumbled my well-planned house of cards. Jacob and my brothers and uncles screamed in me. [They were in hiding in the upper part of the building.] I completely lost control, and out of my mouth issued forth the age-old testament of the eternal Jew: *Shema Yisrael*! Then, in a shocked daze, I felt a hand clasp over my mouth, and the amazed whisper of the connecting words penetrated my ears: *Hashem Elokeinu, Hashem Echad*![181] I spun around to the source of these words, and I found myself looking at Ersabet.

For a moment the world seemed to recede as we stared at each other in mutual shock. Ersabet found her voice first. "You! You of all people!"...

"Nonsense!" I said through chattering teeth. "Stop this right now! My husband, my brothers —five men altogether — are hiding upstairs!"

Ersabet gazed at me in utter shock.... All this transpired under the cover of the blessed uproar, and no one noticed our little drama being played out right under their noses.[182]

Klein protected her husband and brothers who were hiding in the apartment. With her fake Aryan identity, she presented herself in the bomb shelter with the rest of the tenants during air raids, ever careful to hide any evidence that she was not whom she seemed to be and that there were 13 Jews using the apartment as shelter. Her heroism was mostly in the ongoing, day-to-day cover-up that protected her loved ones from the murderous scourge. There were also some singular episodes of heroism, for example, when she walked right into the dreaded Tolonc, from which no Jew ever left, demanding that her father-in-law be released. Miraculously, he was released, with a warning from the head officer: "This is the first and only time that I will let any Jew leave here."[183] The officer explained that the only reason he conceded to her demand was because she "showed [him] a kind of courage that would put a lot of men on the battlefield to shame," and that he couldn't "help but respect courage, even if it is displayed by a Jew."[184]

These examples show Klein protecting the men who are important to her, demonstrating her alliance with the men in her life, as we saw in other religious women's personal narratives. It is because she views herself as a fully able participant in the Jewish community, as we see by her actions, that she is able to feel a complete collusion between Jewish men and women in the struggle to survive. The only time she feels a disparity is when her husband teases her for being so demonstrative toward the baby; she feels that he simply cannot understand her motherly fears of separation.

Klein's gendered experience as a mother seems to foster a feeling of connectedness with mothers of all races, as was demonstrated in the letter Klein wrote to Ersabet. It also fosters a certain disparity between herself as a woman and men, as seen in her feelings of being misunderstood by her husband. On the other hand, her non–gender-specific experience fosters a feeling of connectedness to the Jewish people as a whole, men and women alike. It also fosters — at least it did during the Holocaust — a disparity between herself as a Jew and gentiles.

Another aspect of ultra–Orthodox women's Holocaust testimonials is the use of the transcendent narrative voice, which we saw in Ruchoma Shain's *All for the Boss*. This voice is most distinct in its lack of the qualities we see in much of the writing of *baalot teshuva*: the painful quest for self-discovery and self-transcendence. The transcendent narrative voice does not reveal the narrator's individuality as much as it universalizes the narrator's perceptions. While the *baal teshuva* voice discovers disturbing questions, the transcendent narrative voice formulates mature answers. Indeed, it is the maturity of these authors, similar to the maturity of Shain, that I believe is largely responsible for the self-confident presentation and analysis of personal and public history in these testimonials. We should also remember that Holocaust authors are not *baalot teshuva*. By dint of historical incident, the authors of Holocaust narratives are elderly and were raised as religious Jews from birth. The factors of maturity and settledness in Orthodox life result in the Holocaust authors' different narrative style.

Unlike the confessional, diarist nature of *baal teshuva* narratives, these Holocaust narratives interweave personal accounts with the stories of other figures. They tell history, interspersing retrospection with analysis. The reader feels that the writer posits herself as a representative of her people. Her "I" includes all Jewish women who might have gone through her experience. The inclusivity and universality of the "I" makes it hardly visible as an "I," while the *baal teshuva* "I" is more private and confessional. It is clearly visible as an "I," for the author's quest is her own. Yet it crosses paths with the transcendent narrative "I," which we see in the Holocaust testimonials, because the most private challenges are at the same time universal. As Michel Beaujour explains, the personal narrative's success lies in its speaking for its readers.[185] The transcendent narrative voice and the *baal teshuva* narrative voice speak for ultra–Orthodox women in different ways; however, they unite in their objective to communicate by conflating the readers' and writers' images of the self. The success of Holocaust narratives, like any other personal narrative no matter how different in style, lies in its allowing the reader to imagine herself in the writer's place.

Female Bonding in the Holocaust

Myrna Goldenberg writes that a prevalent theme in general women's Holocaust memoirs is the formation of surrogate families among women for caring and support.[186] Ultra-Orthodox women's Holocaust narratives repeatedly demonstrate the bonding and self-sacrifice that are identified as common phenomena among all women in the Holocaust. The femininity of bonding can be seen in its appearance in Holocaust narratives by both religious and non-religious women.

Since Holocaust sociologists who focus on women's experiences view bonding and mutual caring as qualities that are especially identifiable in women's testimonials, we may conclude that this sort of loving nurturance is female-specific. If so, it would expand the scope of gender-specific experiences among ultra–Orthodox women. I have discussed how religious women authors identify with their people as a whole more than they identify as women, and how sexual exploitation does not appear in their narratives. But if we consider selflessness and bonding to be associated more with women than men in the Holocaust and realize the extensive demonstration of these experiences in religious women's testimonials, then these testimonials can more easily be read as an expression of gendered experiences, at least in part.

The following excerpt demonstrates the author's surprise at an attempt to steal and her conviction that "selflessness and generosity were the norm among the inmates."

> One girl sat on the floor and spread her feet apart. Another girl literally sat in her lap, spreading her legs apart for the next girl. We were crammed together so tightly that we were pinned into place, unable to move our legs or bodies. We were twenty-five hundred girls, packed into a small barracks building....
>
> Absorbed in my thinking, I was surprised to feel a hand groping along the left side of my body. Alarmed and more than a little uncomfortable, I realized that it must be the girl pressed against me. I tried to move away from her, but I couldn't even shift my weight towards the right side. I didn't understand what she could possibly want from me until she tried to reach under my arm. She was reaching for my bread! Somehow, I had held onto that piece of bread distributed at the deportation center in Lodz, a lifetime ago. Had it really been only this morning? Throughout all the confusion and terror, that piece of bread had remained clenched tightly in my fist. Now the girl was trying to reach the bread and take it for herself....
>
> I found out later that the girl had lost her mind when she witnessed the murder of her parents. Actually, an attempt to steal bread was as rare in Auschwitz as a Nazi with a kind heart. Again and again, I saw women handing their bread rations to friends when they thought they were going to their deaths, only to have the bread

returned to them untouched when they miraculously returned to the barracks. Selflessness and generosity were the norm among the inmates. The girl trying to steal my bread was certainly out of the ordinary.[187]

A disturbing question remains in our comparison of general women's Holocaust narratives with those written by ultra–Orthodox women. Why do the religious narratives so conspicuously omit the descriptions of moral degeneration that run throughout general women's testimonials? We have discussed the absence of sexual exploitation or even the fear of it in religious women's narratives. But why the absence of descriptions of the moral degeneration that affected the entire prisoner population in the camps? Admittedly, the women, religious and nonreligious, who have chosen to discuss their Holocaust experiences are not those who epitomize the worst effects of subhuman conditions on human psychology. They are usually the examples of moral heroism. Here, too, we have the uncomfortable problem of taking the women's recollections at face value. We are privy to their subjective views of history, which are usually written long after the events that took place. (Most religious women's narratives were published in the 1990s.)

General women's testimonials recall feats of moral fortitude in the face of unspeakable bestiality, but they are also clear in their descriptions of the psychological and moral degeneration of many ghetto and camp inmates. Religious women's testimonials on the whole lack this dimension. The religiosity of the authors seems to cast a positive hue on their view of history. Their own moral victory is projected onto the Jewish people as a whole. Their own unquestioning faith seems to be possessed by many Jews who went through the Holocaust, according to their descriptions, while general women's testimonials describe events more bleakly and in more morbid detail.[188]

Religious survivor Anna Eilenberg, the author of *Sisters in the Storm*, also co-edited and co-translated (under the name Anna Eilenberg-Eibeshitz) two collections of general women's testimonials. The difference in negative description between the volumes she edited and the one she wrote is pronounced. Her own book lines up with other religious testimonials in its predominance and projection of faith and unwavering morality. However, in the volumes of testimonials she

edited we hear, for example, Mussia Deiches' description of the physical and moral disintegration she witnessed going on around her. She
writes, "Those whose ordinary conduct was uncouth behaved abhor-
rently in the camp. They plunged into a moral abyss and literally turned
into animals." She continues:

> Those who speak of lofty moral achievements in the camps exagger-
> ate. Their words are only hollow rhetoric and do not represent the
> full truth. The Germans were out to crush us, and they succeeded....
> Only a very few unique individuals had the spiritual power to
> remain uncorrupted in those subhuman conditions — and these were
> true angels.[189]

It seems that the recollection of the moral fortitude of Holocaust
victims is colored by the personal experience and convictions of the
teller. In general, the woman of faith sees that faith played out in her
Holocaust experiences. But it is wise to remember that telling history,
especially personal history, is a subjective venture.

CHAPTER NINE

Self-help Literature

Self-help literature is very popular among ultra–Orthodox women. Marriage, homemaking, parenting and emotional maturity are the themes that dominate these books. The overall message is that any woman has the power and freedom of choice to remake much of her physical, emotional, mental and spiritual self; that she is largely responsible for who she is and how she acts. These books stress that one must improve the aspects of life that one can change and positively accept those aspects that one cannot.

The approaches in these books will be familiar to readers of popular psychology. Indeed ultra–Orthodox self-help literature *is* pop psychology, adapted to the needs and outlooks of a religious, Jewish and largely female audience. The most prolific self-help writers, Miriam Adahan and Sarah Chana Radcliffe, are trained therapists with academic backgrounds in psychology. They have adapted their psychological know-how for a religiously observant audience, just as they have adapted their own lives to religious observance.

The following excerpt from a book by Radcliffe demonstrates the extent to which she encourages women to take responsibility for their actions:

> Despite the presence of marital conflict, however, a woman can still strive to fulfill her own Torah obligations, including the laws concerning relations between one's fellow and oneself. These laws pertain directly to her dealings with her husband. Even if he behaves in ways unacceptable to her and contrary to Torah guidelines, she is in no way exempt from behaving in accordance with halachah [Jewish law]. His failure does not provide an excuse for her own failure. Moreover, her only chance for happiness in life is to refuse to fail. She must continue to be her best self for her own sake as well as for

133

the sake of her marriage. If, in the end, it is *Hashem*'s [God's] will that she lacks the power to influence her husband positively, she has the comfort of knowing that she has not transgressed, that she has in fact done all that a wife can do, and that she has earned merit for her efforts.

For this reason, it is valid to write a book on marriage addressed to women only. Although everything contained in this book is equally applicable to men, it is addressed to you, the *aizer k'negdo*.[190] You can take direct control of only your behavior — not your husband's.[191]

This passage points out that Radcliffe is speaking to women. She obviously feels that a female audience is interested in reading a woman-focused book about marriage. She also feels that women's actions can be evaluated and improved independent of men's actions. Radcliffe is not telling women how to manipulate husbands, even though she believes that through her actions a woman has the power to influence her husband. She is telling women how to be the best wives possible, referring to them as whole people, not just as half of a consecrated partnership. In this way, she accords women the full extent of their control in marriage. If a woman is dependent upon the actions of her husband or accountable for them, then her own scope of action is crippled: A woman's actions become male-centered, focused on how each move helps or hinders positive or negative responses in her mate.

Radcliffe urges women to look at themselves as individuals. This encourages emotional maturity, a sense of responsibility for one's right behavior despite an abundance of reasonable justifications and provocations to behave otherwise. It also encourages a sense of control, an awareness that a woman can and should perform an action because it is right, even if it produces an undesirable (or desirable) response from her husband. Radcliffe's method assumes the existence of an ethical touchstone in the married couple's life, a nondebatable gauge for behavioral and moral correctness. Jewish law and tradition play this role.

The existence of a code of ethics and actions serves as a reference point and boundary marker in marital life. It ensures that an action can only be correct toward one's spouse as long as it is also correct toward God; that an action or attitude can only be called right in the marriage if it is right according to Judaism. It also includes the possibility that what "feels right" may not *be* right. An external value system ensures that neither sex is exclusively dependent upon the other as an absolute referent for evaluating the virtue or vice of a particular habit. A partner in such a marriage would tend to view herself as ultimately accountable to God for her actions, which confers a sense of responsibility and control over oneself. After all, if one believes she is accountable for her behavior, she will be more concerned with how she *acts* than with why she *reacts*. She will be more concerned with modifying her behavior than justifying it and more aware of her individuality within the marriage — as a whole entity who is half of a larger whole.

Psychologist Miriam Adahan's books largely focus on taking control of life by taking control of one's emotional/mental state. Her books are replete with examples and techniques for reprogramming one's destructive thoughts into more positive ones.

> What we do or do not value is a matter of culture and innate personality traits. A tone-deaf person, for example, will not value music as a musician does. A small child cannot appreciate religious values as one who has studied for many years.
>
> What we value can also change in an instant. For example, if someone showed you a diamond and said that it was of the highest quality, worth millions of dollars, you would look at it as something of great value. Then if an expert came along and said it was a fake, suddenly it would just be a fancy piece of glass, no longer of value.
>
> You can use the real diamond/fake diamond analogy in your life. You may have given some things real diamond value which don't deserve to be valued, such as certain people's negative opinions or having status based on material wealth. You can change this in an instant.
>
> You are the jeweler of your life. You decide what's glass and what's a real jewel. This switch in perception is not as difficult as you may think. As you've grown older, you've discarded many things which you thought were of value when you were younger, and later realized were worthless. If you are a *ba'al teshuvah*, you saw your values change radically, in a relatively short period of time. Before becoming Observant, you valued certain politicians or movie stars, possessions, concepts and books which are no longer of value to you. Now you value learning, family, discipline, *chesed* [loving kindness], modesty, etc. You were able to make a major change in what you valued and what you did not.
>
> You can use the same power to minimize critical remarks and minor disappointments. You can use the same power to maximize the beauty, love, and many blessings in your life.[192]

Adahan's methodology is not original, but her incorporation of Torah ideals is. She clearly writes to a religious Jewish audience, assuming that her examples of values will ring true; values such as the negativity of "having status based on material wealth" or her depiction of the *baal teshuva* who has changed many of his values.

Adahan does not address only women, but it seems that the majority of her cases and concerns better suit female readers. She certainly speaks to women in her article "Feeling Worthwhile — With or Without a Man," in which she urges women to rely on themselves for fulfillment, not to wait around for men to give it to them, which quite likely won't happen. She points to negative socialization, which feminism condemned decades ago, as the root cause of women's unhealthy psychological orientation: "Women are socialized that to be 'needy,' weak, shy and unassertive is 'feminine'.... She is trained to please 'him'—whoever that might be."[193] It sounds feminist, which should not be surprising considering the issues we've already seen in ultra–Orthodox women's writing, issues that are readily apparent as feminist concerns. However, Adahan's blaming of "nurture" for women's unhealthy psyche is puzzling, especially considering the emphasis that Michael Kaufman placed on natural gender differences and his detailed collection of evidence to that effect. Adahan's viewpoint is understandable; what is baffling is its exclusivity: She blames *only* socialization for the inequality in male and female self-images in this article. It is troublesome that one religious advocate could unequivocally impute "nature" for the differences between men and women and one "nurture." Why the disparity? And is one way of thinking more authentically Jewish than the other?

When we look at the differences between Adahan's and Kaufman's approaches, two things become clear. One is that Kaufman is speaking about natural, not necessarily negative, differences between men and women; differences such as women's prevalence in caretaking professions even when the society (supposedly) did not encourage it, such as in early kibbutz life. His point is that women naturally tend to choose certain roles that we think of as female roles, and that is because of their innate gender difference. He also points to scientific studies on brain hemisphere functioning to support his argument that Judaism's claim for inherent gender differences is empirically founded. However, Adahan is speaking about negative differences, differences that are psychologically destructive to women. It is hard to envision that women, as a result of their gender, "naturally" choose self-destructive patterns. But considering the conclusions of decades of feminist inquiry, we can easily envision a society that socializes women to follow destructive patterns, so that when discussing unhealthy psychological patterns in women, blaming socialization simply makes more sense. But does it make sense Jewishly? Does Jewish law accommodate the concept of negative socialization, as Kaufman claims that it accommodates the idea of inherent gender differences?

Throughout works and discussions of Jewish law there are remarks about customs that are antithetical to the spirit of Judaism; comments about societal practice that mistakenly became the norm: a *minhag pasul*, an improper custom. Also the whole thrust of the *Mussar* movement in Judaism stressed the individual's responsibility to recondition one's actions and thoughts. Changing one's negative character traits, *middos*, is considered imperative to spiritual growth, albeit difficult. The concept of "working on your *middos*," an ethical imperative, means that Judaism holds that with hard work one can resocialize oneself, create new habits and thought patterns. It follows from this that Judaism admits the possibility of negative socialization. We can therefore assume that there is at least nothing wrong in terms of Jewish thought with blaming detrimental female differences on socialization.

All the same, Adahan's perspective neatly lines up with feminism. She is aware of this and presents a curious disclaimer: "To those who may accuse me of 'women's lib,' I assure you that the foregoing is not an attempt to make man-haters out of women."[194] Her association of the women's movement with man hating clearly shows its negative associations in her mind — or at least in the minds of her readers who she fears would "accuse" her of it. Ironically, this article could not possibly sound more feminist, more pro women's independence, more anti "waiting   waiting for a man to marry her, waiting for a man to give her meaning, waiting for a man to take the initiative to make her feel wanted, loved and worthwhile, and to give her orders which she carries out submissively."[195]

The thrust of Adahan's argument complements Radcliffe's: Women must be responsible for and in control of their attitudes and actions. She again echoes Radcliffe when she asserts the need for women to envision themselves and act as whole individuals: "A healthy relationship requires two 'whole' people, not one whole and one half, with the latter waiting in resentment, bitterness or anxiety for the former to give her purpose."[196] Adahan's accusers, if they ever materialized, did not affect her popularity in ultra–Orthodox circles very much, for her article "Feeling Worthwhile — With or Without a Man" was reprinted in the premier Israel issue of *Bat Kol: Jewish Women's Journal*.[197]

We have discussed how the literature produced by ultra–Orthodox women writers is largely reactionary, a spontaneous response to the influence of feminism, which is viewed by ultra–Orthodox proponents as a threat to Jewish values. We have discussed examples of the literature's preoccupation with redressing feminist thought. Adahan clearly demonstrates a resistance to feminism that is contradictory: She nominally condemns feminist ideals while clearly utilizing feminist paradigms. She frames her arguments in the terms of feminist independence, displaying a well-integrated feminist consciousness, despite her questionable disclaimer. We can agree that her thesis of female independence to encourage psychological health has the goal of enhancing the observance of Judaism. But, just as she freely adopts psychological techniques and concepts to enhance religious Jewish practice, we can safely assume that she also adopts feminist concepts to the same end. The interesting difference is that feminism is viewed with a certain amount of contempt. This should not be surprising at this point in the research and simply signifies that feminism may be Adahan's and ultra–Orthodox women's "madwoman in the attic," a suppressed, undesirable feminine "delinquency" that surfaces occasionally to reveal what its very denial cannot deny: the extent of its influence.[198] The significance of the madwoman's suppression is that it demonstrates the ambivalent or negative image of feminism in ultra–Orthodox women's minds.

CHAPTER TEN

Fiction

There is not a great deal of difference between much of the fiction and nonfiction in ultra–Orthodox English-language women's literature. It is often impossible to distinguish whether certain works are fiction or nonfiction unless the reader is told.

The fiction strives to be as realistic, as true-to-life as nonfiction. Works of fiction often closely imitate nonfiction styles such as diaries and autobiographies. Experimental or fantastic fiction is nonexistent. And, unlike general women's literature, heavy melodrama and tragedy are unpopular. We may again draw upon Michel Beaujour's conclusions that the success of the self-portrait is in its speaking for its readers and that there is a conflation of the writer and reader of a popular self-portrait. In other words, in hearing the author's voice, we are hearing the reader's voice as well. If we apply this theory to ultra–Orthodox women's fiction (since it imitates personal narrative style), we may conclude that nonrealistic (experimental or fantastic) fiction is unavailable because it is not appealing to the ultra–Orthodox reader. This analysis is helpful, but we will see that it is only true to a limited extent, because ultra–Orthodox women's fiction also has its detractors from within its own camp.

We will find that many works of fiction treat the women's issues that we saw in the personal narratives. What *is* popular in fiction, then, is personal power and heroism; the inspiration that is called upon to succeed in times of difficulty. This body of fiction suggests that ultra–Orthodox women are interested in writing and reading works that move them emotionally. They want to be inspired, to read books that are testimony to the indomitability of the human spirit and the ever-present hand of God in the play of events.

Do the above descriptions, which define popular ultra–Orthodox fiction (and nonfiction, for that matter), also define it as "literature"? This question must be asked only insofar as some ultra–Orthodox women are asking it of themselves. Art can be found in just about any form, so the pulling out of interesting literary threads in the sections that follow does not mean that, as a whole, ultra–Orthodox women's fiction is deemed good literature by its readers. My analysis of this fiction focuses on its cultural significance more than its literary significance so, for our purposes, it is rich. But hearing several times from different religious women that religious women's writing is not "literature" is also a culturally significant factor.[199] I bring up the issue here because fiction is clearly the least developed of all categories of nonacademic, religious Jewish writing (i.e., writing that is dominated by women).

On one hand, the existing ultra–Orthodox fiction must satisfy enough readers to make it marketable, and, indeed, works of religious fiction are found in most English-speaking religious homes. On the other hand, the fiction available does not satisfy the aesthetic sensibilities of every reader. Saying that religious Jewish writing is not "literature" implies that it is not subtle or sophisticated enough, critical theory aside. It also says that it is not imaginative enough, creative enough, or that it lacks profundity, which is especially relevant where fiction is concerned. It is hard to judge how widespread this feeling is, but works of fiction have not attained the popularity of some nonfictive personal narratives.

One explanation for the opinion of those critics from within the Orthodox fold is that much of religious women's prose is written by amateurs. The authors whose works we have examined so far and will examine are for the most part not professional writers, but they are women who write well and have something to say. They are women with a message for other women, and in such cases, expressive ability might be important, but it is subordinate to the gift of inspiring others. The inspiration, the message, is the goal.

The writers of Holocaust testimonials are also not professional writers by and large. Much writing in the self-help category is written by experienced writers, but few readers have high artistic expectations from self-help books. Even the personal narratives are not usually written by professional writers. In the anthologies, we looked at texts whose whole impact was based on the message and perspective of the writer and not on the writer's art per se.

In her introduction to *Our Lives*, Sarah Shapiro tells about her part in reviving a friend's buried literary talent. In her introduction to *More of Our Lives* and in *Don't You Know It's a Perfect World?*, she writes about the experience of women in a writing workshop sharing their writings with other women. The experience of sharing fresh, undeveloped writing is one that she relates to; it appeals to her, and, no doubt, it is one of the purposes of the ultra–Orthodox women's anthologies she edits. This literature in general acts as a forum for sharing bits of inspiration wrapped in well-chosen words. It often reads like a monthly newsletter from an amateur writers' workshop. They have something to tell one another, and they love to tell it in words, which is why they write.

This is quite different from professional writers who view themselves as artists whose raw material is words. In literary history, we often see writers — literary craftspeople — whose writing consists of a few repetitive themes — and not very soul-stirring ones either. But their skill in unfolding a scene to the senses, divulging a character's startling secret or giving the plot a shock treatment is as aesthetically fresh each time as the introduction of yet a new strain of hybrid tea rose. This obsession with aesthetics is foreign to ultra–Orthodox Jewish writing but is supplanted by concerns with meaning, content, inspiration and message.

Thus, the divergence of ultra–Orthodox fiction from general fiction is in its goal orientation. Or, we may say that the fact that a literature is valued primarily for its goal (i.e., the expression of Torah ideals in various forms) distinguishes it from a literature that is valued primarily for its method (i.e., its literary artistry).

Ideologically focused fiction possesses an advantage for us as critics: Its cultural foundations are more transparent. Religious women's fiction, in its attempt to impart messages of inspiration to its readers, makes clear the societal framework that defines what is inspiring. In sketching heroines whose actions preach moral lessons, it reveals the morals on which those lessons are based.

Another reason why some religious women readers might complain that there is no good religious women's fiction is because their reading tastes were shaped by a culture that is different than the one in which they presently take part.[200] *Baalot teshuva* can pick up any number of nonfictive religious women's works with no disappointment.

There are any number of well-written personal narratives, biographies and self-help books. But when it comes to fiction, too much of what she reads may seem predictable, clichéd, trite or simply too narrow. What she is really looking for is a dramatic page-turner with some unexpected, imaginative plot, scenes and characters. She is looking for the fiction she was used to in her secular days, where a good read was an artistic, engaging experience and "the moral of the story" was what you left behind with your kindergarten teacher.

The *baalat teshuva*— or any religious woman who has drunk deeply from secular, Western literature — may find that she turned away from that literature because of its ethical vacancy, its lack of Torah ideals and morals in general. But while ultra–Orthodox women's fiction may contain the moral ideology that speaks to her current sensibilities, it cannot fulfill her aesthetic expectations, which were cultivated by a culture she no longer wishes to be part of.

Marge Piercy's *He, She and It* presents an interesting contrast with ultra–Orthodox women's fiction.[201] This novel is a work of science fiction, but Piercy intersperses an imaginative reenactment of the story of the Maharal of Prague, a brilliant sixteenth-century Jewish leader and kabbalist. The heroine is a woman of the future, after the world was nearly destroyed. She interacts with an "it," the first successful manmade "human." This "it" is set parallel to the Maharal's historical Golem, a "man" he created through practical kabbalah to help the oppressed Jews in his time. The novel is a fascinating read and shows an impressive use of imagination both in pure invention and historical dramatization. The striking thing is that the Maharal of Prague is an ultra–Orthodox Jewish paragon and has been the subject of ultra–Orthodox nonfiction. As such he could easily be made the subject of fiction, too. And here he is, the subject of a non–ultra–Orthodox writer's imaginative powerhouse of a book, which makes ultra–Orthodox women's fiction look utterly sterile in comparison.

I purposely do not pit other so-called "Orthodox" Jewish fiction, such as that of Naomi Ragen, against ultra–Orthodox women's fiction. Ultra-Orthodox readers view this fiction as a mistreatment of religious Jewish themes, a misrepresentation of their community and an overplaying of its aberrations. It is simply not condoned reading in ultra–Orthodox Jewish circles. Piercy's book is also not circulated among ultra–Orthodox women readers, but the difference is that Piercy is not one of the "Orthodox" writers. Her work does not aim to represent the contemporary ultra–Orthodox world. Her heroine is quite secular in all respects and acts accordingly, while her representation of the Maharal of Prague in the sixteenth century imagines and respects the proper religiosity of the Jews at that time. There is no playing up of characters who got hurt by or don't fit into the system, so it is not threatening to ultra–Orthodoxy's self-image.

We can understand why ultra–Orthodoxy would not use "Orthodox" women's fiction as a prototype for its own fiction. The question is: Why don't we see in ultra–Orthodox women's fiction the sort of creativity and originality that Piercy is able to infuse into a valid Jewish subject? On a closer look, there are several reasons why *He, She and It* is not and could never be the product of an ultra–Orthodox woman's pen, reasons that are important to our understanding of the limitations we see in ultra–Orthodox women's literature.

The first big limitation is modesty. Ultra-Orthodoxy's strict standard of modesty precludes the type of sexually driven interactions that significantly add to *He, She and It*. Piercy's novel does not exist for male/female relationships, as many novels do. Yet the sort of excitement added to a novel by including this aspect is not to be underrated. Ultra-Orthodox women's fiction, in effectively neutering its characters, must provide a lot more in the way of interesting character and plot development. This simple difference probably accounts for more than we realize.

The other consideration has to do with religious sentiments. If an ultra–Orthodox woman were to write the sort of dramatic reenactment of the Maharal's story that Piercy did, she would have to be very bold and perhaps not too wise. The Maharal as a paragon of ultra–Orthodox scholarship and piety is almost untouchable as the subject of a "good story." Such fiction in the ultra–Orthodox world would be prone to the highest scrutiny. Could a writer faithfully commit herself to dramatizing the Maharal of Prague, to reconstructing his lofty thoughts, without insulting her readers' religious sentiments and making herself a laughingstock? An ultra–Orthodox model who has been thoroughly documented cannot be easily adapted into a fictionalized narrative. As a non–ultra–Orthodox writer, Piercy does not possess this sensitivity or this limitation. While she does not express hostility toward traditional Judaism, as other supposedly "Orthodox" writers may, she also freely and successfully fictionalizes and improvises her character and his thoughts. An ultra–Orthodox writer would not take this liberty lightly.

We will discuss several cases of dramatizations of historical figures, including Shoshana Lepon's *No Greater Treasure* and the anonymously published *And Rachel Was His Wife*.[202] We will see that in these cases the authors employ techniques that allow them to imaginatively, but cautiously, reproduce great historical characters. Each of the stories in *No Greater Treasure* is quite short, allowing Lepon to stay relatively within the bounds of the scanty documentation provided by her sources. *And Rachel Was His Wife* dramatizes the time of the great Mishnaic scholar Rabbi Akiva. Rachel, his wife, is the heroine of the story but not the narrator. Rachel's fictive friend narrates the story, and this distance from the true-life heroine grants the author more freedom of description and ascription.

Historical Fiction

The publishers of Rosalie Lamet's *City of Diamonds* call it a "dramatization of her own true story." It is an autobiographical novel, so it falls in the category of fiction, yet it sounds exactly like many other personal narratives about the Holocaust. *City of Diamonds* straddles the fence between fiction and nonfiction, demonstrating the general feature of ultra–Orthodox fiction to be utterly realistic, if not virtually true. It also contains the heroism that we find throughout the Holocaust testimonials.

In *City of Diamonds*, a young religious woman from a well-to-do Belgian home undergoes upheaval and hardship under the Nazi occupation. The most dramatic part of this upheaval is what occurs in her own person. She was spoiled, the narrator admits, extremely overprotected and pampered by a doting mother. She found herself unready to marry when the matchmaker insisted she meet men for marriage and unready to part from her mother's side when her safety depended upon it. Yet not only does the narrator overcome her fears and take leave of her family, she becomes a guide for four Dutch Jews, smuggling them and herself across to Free France on a trip fraught with danger. Here she sees the first revelation of her true self:

Suddenly, I was no longer afraid that those in the compartment would suspect that I, too, was Jewish. I cried out, "Lies! You're repeating nothing but the trumped-up vicious lies you've been fed! It's people like you who poison it for everyone!"

The woman stared at me blankly. She seemed taken aback by my outburst. Just then, the train slowed to a stop. The woman stood up with her newspaper tucked under her arm. She hissed, "The time is coming when every true Fleming shall wake up and worship the *Fuhrer. Heil Hitler!*"

Then she was gone. Long after she had left and the collective muttering in the train had abated I trembled and had trouble swallowing. My tongue seemed paralyzed. Had that been *me* shouting back at the woman? Quiet little Naomi? I wondered at my fearlessness.[203]

As the narrator finally arrives with the Dutch Jews at the station to board the train taking them to freedom, she discovers selfhood, maturity and a spiritual connection to a higher goal: future generations.

A strange sensation came over me, something I had never experienced before. I had the oddest feeling that each step I was taking was not only bringing me closer to freedom but toward the forming of a whole person — me. For the first time I felt a complete readiness to marry and bring other souls into the world. Fantastically, I could almost sense those souls hovering about me, beckoning me: "Come, Naomi, step lively. So much depends on you. Come forward, so we, too, can be born."[204]

In the above passage, reproduction is associated with the narrator's feeling of wholeness and maturity. The juxtaposition of the concern for bearing children with the narrator's sense of personal safety is reminiscent of a similar, but converse, theme in general women's Holocaust testimonials, where a fear of sterility accompanies the sense of personal danger.[205] It is ironic that the fear of sterility or the yearning to bear children does not often appear in religious women's testimonials, but it does find its way into this fictionalized Holocaust narrative written by a religious woman.

The *Pomegranate Pendant: A Historical Novel* is as much "historical" as "novel." The fictional part of this story is woven into the factual history of Jerusalem of the last century. Yet the author, Dvora

Waysman, stresses the realistic, factual aspects of this story so much that the fictional plot is weak; the heroine/narrator of the story mostly tells history. This novel is packed with historical facts and figures, with not very much happening to not very many people.

In this book about Yemenite and other Jewish ethnic groups' immigration to old Jerusalem, we see the infiltration of women's issues in an incongruous way. Waysman creates a narrator who is a traditional Yemenite woman from a traditional Yemenite family. It is surprising that she stands out among other female Yemenites of her generation as being progressive. It seems that Waysman has imposed feminist values of women's financial and social independence on her character. For example, her heroine, after being widowed, gains financial independence when she decides to purchase a second house and create and sell her own crafts, all things that a woman of her culture and generation would not normally have done. The narrator also stands firm in her decision never to remarry after being widowed at the age of 22. (She was married at 14, which was customary. Remaining single after widowhood was not.) She teaches herself to read and becomes fluent in many languages. The women of her generation were illiterate; literacy was considered masculine and unseemly for a woman. Here, the narrator/heroine, Mazal, speaks with her friend Sarah, who is older and comes from a more Westernized background:

> Sarah clapped her hands with delight. "My little friend," she said in wonder, "what other hidden talents do you possess?"
> "None, I'm afraid," I answered shyly. "I memorize as much as I can from your books because I am afraid that the new facts I read about will escape from me, and I'll revert to being the ignorant girl who arrived in Jerusalem a decade ago."
> Sarah was silent for a while. "I think," she said after a pause, "that if you'd been born in a different place, perhaps in a different time, you could have been a great scholar or perhaps played a role in the history of this country." ... "But I'm just a woman...," I began.
> Sarah shook her head. "Chavah [Eve] was just a woman — the mother of all creation. Sarah, Rivkah [Rebecca], Rachel, and Leah were all just women. Devorah the Prophetess was just a woman. I don't think you realize how remarkable you are."[206]

This passage demonstrates a narrative strategy that is uncommon for the literature we are reviewing. Susan Sniader Lanser in *Fictions of Authority: Women Writers and Narrative Voice* shows how much of Western literature by women uses various strategies of narrative voice to mask the author's "authority." This, she claims, is because "women writers' adoption of overt authoriality has usually meant transgressing gendered rhetorical codes."[207] Lanser shows how narrative strategies may conceal the authority of the author, as if she is afraid of her disqualification, by giving that authority to one of her characters.

The above passage from *The Pomegranate Pendant*, for example, is narrated by Mazal, the main heroine whose actions are progressive for her time. Sarah is an auxiliary character in the plot, a character who is *expected* to be more progressive because of her Western, *Ashkenazi* background. It is Sarah, twice-removed in importance from the author, who is given the narrative authority, or burden, of pointing out the unconventionality of the heroine. This is unusual in ultra–Orthodox women's fiction. Narration is usually straightforward, with each male or female character responsible and unapologetic for his or her own actions. If we use Lanser's paradigm, we might understand that the authorial voice wishes to conceal her own womanly authority and therefore grants it to a character who is more removed from herself and her first-person narrator. But, considering that subversive narrative strategies in this fiction are unlikely and unintentional, it is more probable that the author wishes to *reveal* Mazal's achievements but cannot make her sound too progressive or too feminist because it would not be realistic. As we have seen, realism is an overt concern of the literature, as is female empowerment. There is no reason for the author to conceal her "authority"; it is quite apparent throughout the text. If anything, the author's concern with female empowerment is too apparent and takes away from the realism that the novel tries to attain.

Throughout the book, we see the incongruity of a conscientiously factual depiction of history being narrated by a woman who is atypically progressive for her status and time. Historical documentation is overlaid with the strange fiction of a woman remaking herself. The narrator never throws off the yoke of her beliefs and is full of faith to her core, but she does not continue practices that negatively affect women (though she continues to obey Jewish law). The scenario is meant to be progressive. Yet, for all its concern with realism as a historical novel, there is a categorical intrusion of the author's contemporary feminist concerns.

And Rachel Was His Wife is another historical novel, published anonymously and revised and edited by Marsi Tabak of Feldheim Publishers. Like *The Pomegranate Pendant*, this book is very concerned with historical accuracy, stressing the telling of history rather than the movement of the characters within it.

And Rachel Was His Wife differs from *The Pomegranate Pendant* in the way it confers heroism upon its characters. The Yemenite narrator/ heroine of *The Pomegranate Pendant* is heroic according to the contemporary, feminist standard of female independence. Modern women influenced by feminist issues can easily identify with her brand of heroism. Yet, as I stated above, a character who comes from a society of female dependency and quickly achieves personal independence is unrealistic. However, it does show the concern of the ultra–Orthodox woman writer with women's personal power.

The anonymous author of *And Rachel Was His Wife* attempts to impart a realistic depiction of the heroism of Rachel, wife of the renowned Mishnaic sage Rabbi Akiva, who lived 2,000 years ago. Rachel is heroic according to a traditional Jewish standard of female piety. That standard is discernible in the following Talmudic passage and is the basis for the heroism of the historically factual character of Rachel: "Why are women selected for special merit [from God, greater than the merit of men]? Because they take their children to the synagogue to study Torah, they motivate their husbands to study Torah by allowing them time in the House of Study, and they wait up for their husbands to return from the House of Study, and they allow them to go and study Torah in another city."[208] This is certainly not the paragon of womanhood in feminist terms, but it is in keeping with the Jewish maxim *Gadol ham'aseh yoter mi-ha'oseh.*[209] Or, as Michael Kaufman translates, "Greater is the one who causes a good deed to be performed than the one who actually does it."[210]

The greatness of Rachel is in Jewish terms, as the role of the enabler is glorified in Judaism. Rachel saw Akiva's potential when he was an ignorant shepherd, and she nurtured that spark of greatness until he became a Torah sage unequaled in stature. Her heroism is largely passive: She allowed him to "go and study Torah in another city," while she chose to live in abject poverty, forgoing her right to be financially supported. Rachel, the daughter of one of the richest men of ancient Israel, sacrificed material comforts so that her husband could study Torah all day long. This is the historical scenario from the Talmud.

The main fictional character in *And Rachel Was His Wife* is Rachel's friend, who narrates the story. It is through the narrator's eyes that the heroism of a woman about whom little is told in the Talmud is glorified. The author's agenda is to recuperate the acclaimed, yet elusive, figure of Rachel, to imaginatively expound upon the historical atmosphere in which she lived. What happens, interestingly enough, is that from the passive heroism of the pious Jewish woman sending her husband off to study, we see the active heroism of her impact upon the lives of other women. The fictional narrator describes how Rachel's self-sacrifice influenced her to encourage her own husband and sons to study Torah, which in turn fostered her own appreciation of Torah scholarship and practice.

Why did the author create a fictional narrator to tell the story of the nonfictional heroine? Perhaps because the task of Rachel narrating her own story is too daunting. She is, after all, a traditional Jewish heroine. The author bears a great burden in trying to do justice to her ancestor, in not assigning her the wrong thoughts or speech. Instead, the author created a narrator who was influenced by Rachel and also witnessed the events of the time. When she first begins her story, this narrator is a relatively simple young girl with a proclivity to babbling and materialism. It is certainly easier for us to relate to this fictional narrator than to spend a whole book inside the mind of a character who is exceptionally elevated. It also allows for entertainment, which may not have been possible if the narrator were the embodiment of religious devotion.

In the following passage, the narrator tells us about the conflicting thoughts she has during a visit to Rachel. She first compares herself to the heroine and fares badly. She then compares herself to her and Rachel's friend, Shifra, who has drifted away from traditional Jewish practices, assimilating into Roman society. She fares better. Not only does the passage give us a taste of the atmosphere of the time, but it amuses us:

> I'm only a year older than Rachel and my life has been easy; first my parents always protected me, even spoiled me, and then my husband took over. And what are my worries? That a child has a sniffle? That my maid will leave me? That Elazar spends too much time in the

house of study, and not enough at home or in the business? Nobody should have it worse, *beli ayin hara*! And yet, I feel that, compared to Rachel, I look old. Of course, I'm a bit overweight — I've learned to be a very good cook now, and I really enjoy it. And what with our frequent visitors — traveling scholars, business guests and so on — I'm preparing more elaborate meals. How would I know if a recipe is good unless I taste it? Sometimes it takes a lot of tasting to get the seasoning just right.

Anyway, I'd rather be a bit heavy than gaunt like Shifra. She's absolutely determined to stay young-looking forever. There was a time when I suspected that she used the vomitorium regularly — all the Roman matrons were doing it. They'd eat and eat until they were stuffed and then disgorge everything. That way, they were able to try all the new dishes, indulge themselves day and night, yet never gain a *sela*. But no Jewish woman — no matter how assimilated — would do such a disgusting thing. She's as thin as ever though, and she eats twice as much as I do. Maybe she's had a tapeworm inserted — that's the latest.[211]

Impelling this book is a desire to tangibly know Rachel, that woman in the Talmud about whom Rabbi Akiva, the once-ignorant shepherd returning after 24 years of intense Torah study with 24,000 pupils, said, "Mine and yours is hers."[212] Rachel is credited with the spiritual merit of her husband's and his pupils' Torah study. This book is the manifestation of the yearning of ultra–Orthodox women to *know* a woman who is heroic because she gave of herself completely for the study of sacred Jewish works.

The aspiration to write a book such as *And Rachel Was His Wife* is the same as that which compelled Shoshana Lepon to write *No Greater Treasure: Stories of Extraordinary Women Drawn from the Talmud and Midrash*. In similar style, Lepon imaginatively dramatizes historic female figures in Jewish history, drawing on often vague or incomplete details that she gleans from traditional Jewish sources. The result is a glorification of these women for their piety, charity, faith and wisdom. They are celebrated for their achievements by Jewish standards, which are not always congruent with feminist prototypes of success. However, by all standards, the heroism of the women in Lepon's stories lies in their capacity to influence people and circumstances. All these women have personal power and the wisdom to use it to the best advantage.

In both *And Rachel Was His Wife* and *No Greater Treasure*, we are witnessing the literary counterpart to the critical activity that Tamar Frankiel espouses and practices in *The Voice of Sarah: Feminine Spirituality and Traditional Judaism*. Frankiel encourages the recovery of feminine dimensions from within Jewish sources, a rereading of the stories of great Jewish women.[213] By dramatizing the stories, reenacting them and filling in the gaps, the authors are using the contemporary imagination to recuperate the lives of historic Jewish women. This allows the readers of this literature to place themselves inside those stories and actively recover feminine aspects that speak to religious women today. In this way, historical novels in ultra–Orthodox literature, especially when they expound on the lives of real women of the past, help to reclaim for contemporary Jewish women role models who are grounded in their own traditions.

Contemporary Fiction

The historical works we have reviewed all treat issues of women's empowerment in one way or another, even though these themes are usually subordinate to the historical documentation. Ultra-Orthodox fiction that is set in the present-day is mostly written by women and mostly deals with issues related to women, such as domesticity, religiosity, human relationships and personal development. This does not sound much different from general women's fiction except for a few crucial points.

Human relationships in ultra–Orthodox fiction do not necessarily begin with heterosexual romance or dating and end with marriage, as we so often see in general women's fiction. There *is* courtship, but it is usually in the modest ultra–Orthodox style of *shidduchim*, in which a man and woman (or their parents) find suitable partners for marriage by consulting a matchmaker or other third party. Each side of the intended partnership checks out the other side indirectly by gleaning information from people who know the intended partner and his family. The couple then meet several times to conclude for themselves (or agree with their parents) that they could indeed create a suitable marriage. The goal of a date is always marriage, never romance, although it doesn't necessarily preclude the possibility of nonphysical romance.

This scenario is not only true fictionally but culturally. Marriage is a religious obligation for men and a natural desire of women, Jewish sources tell us. A single person is considered half a person, unable to complete himself without a marriage partner. This means that marriage always remains a force to be reckoned with. Singleness is viewed as a temporary state. The Jewish outlook is that personal development is incomplete outside the framework of marriage.

For women, this has significant ramifications, for marriage *a priori* means children, certainly in the ultra–Orthodox mind. If children do not come, there will most likely be a lot of emotional turmoil to deal with. If they do come, there may also be a lot of emotional turmoil. And this would most likely be the case with *baalot teshuva*, who were not usually raised in large families and are unfamiliar with their running. They were also most likely raised to be single-mindedly ambitious about their careers. Emotional turmoil may arise when they discover that motherhood is not conducive to anything other than single-minded mothering, rarely providing the intellectual stimulation to which they were accustomed. Issues of career versus homemaking are prevalent in the fiction.

We can therefore understand how domesticity in general women's fiction and in ultra–Orthodox fiction is different. First, as we discussed before, domesticity is connected with religiosity. For a woman, homemaking and raising children are seen as her way of serving God. Second, domesticity is unsettling to the *baalat teshuva*, more so than to women who were raised in religious homes. It is the arena in which she expresses her religiosity and the arena in which she must compromise career ambitions the most. It is a compromise fraught with conflict: There is nothing Jewishly wrong with realizing fulfillment in career success, but it does not compare ideologically to mothering, which is connected to holiness. Motherhood is her way of connecting to other religious women and expressing the giving that is idealized in her society. On the other hand, a successful career can satisfy intellectual and ego needs. Mothering is not conducive to satisfying those needs and can be emotionally burdensome. The career/homemaking conflict is further complicated by two other factors: The ultra–Orthodox style of mothering, i.e., natural reproduction, which can result in many children, makes working outside the home especially difficult, and many mothers *must* work outside the home to make ends meet. Throw all these difficulties together, it is understandable how career ambitions can provide grist for conflict and, therefore, grist for the making of an ultra–Orthodox novel, especially a novel with a heroine who is a *baalat teshuva*.

In Rachel Pomerantz's *A Time to Rend, a Time to Sew*, we meet Beth Snyder and her family. At a young age, she was influenced by her father, a doctor, to push to the top of the social ladder. To him that meant becoming a surgeon. As a Jewish woman, she faces prejudice along the way and overcomes each obstacle with the fire of her ambition. She is brilliant, she is hard working, and she is consumed by an ambition to be the best. The first conflict arises when she decides to take on Jewish practices, including keeping *Shabbos*. She then becomes upset with herself when she does not keep the Sabbath under the pressure of an upcoming test.

> She had been faced with a straightforward conflict between her ambitions and her Jewishness, and of course her ambitions had won. She had been trained since she was a little girl to succeed, and the more opposition she had run into, the more determined she had grown. To try to withstand that stubborn determination with vague feelings about the sanctity of Shabbos was like trying to stop a cannonball with a lace curtain.
>
> Beth plodded along the sidewalk. Why did she have to be so single-minded? Why couldn't she have a private life? The men at the Hillel House services didn't seem to suffer from these conflicts, regardless of their chosen field of study. Was it their maleness that enabled them to indulge themselves? She didn't mind sacrificing comfort to become a doctor, but why did she have to turn her back on every other interest in order to succeed? How high was the price of having been born a girl?
>
> Beth stopped walking. She couldn't aim lower; her conscience wouldn't let her. But why not aim higher? Why not try to make it to the top without sacrificing her commitment to Judaism?... It would be a tremendous challenge, but Beth thrived on challenges.[214]

Slowly, as her commitment to Judaism holds firm alongside her unwavering ambition to become a surgeon, a crack begins to form in her whole mental construct. She spends part of her last year of medical school in a university hospital in Jerusalem. During that time, she agrees to go out with a rabbinical student, despite her conviction that marriage would interfere with her career at this point. It turns out, however, that he is very personable and intelligent, just the sort of man she would like to marry — but not now. It is he, who has already eschewed the secular American world for the ultra–Orthodox one, who challenges her to examine the basis of her ambitions. In the end, she refuses to marry him.

Here, we see the real issue of the novel. More than a question of career ambitions versus the desire to marry and raise a family, the novel forces us to question the source of our ambitions. We sense this question from the beginning, as Pomerantz opens the novel with a quotation from Ecclesiastes 4:4,6: "And I saw that all labor and all skillful enterprise spring from man's rivalry with his neighbor. This, too, is futility and a vexation of the spirit!... Better is one handful of tranquillity, than two fistfuls of labor and frustration."

Which person and which society will dictate to us what is the top? And why do we need to get there? With these questions, ultra–Orthodox fiction takes us one step beyond general fiction. Traditional Judaism offers a different set of values, a different possible combination of ambitions that are esteemed by its different culture. Beth is challenged by a man who has indeed chosen to adopt the ambitions of ultra–Orthodox Jewish culture:

> She swung around to face him directly. "Absolutely not!" she exploded. "For years I have sacrificed sleep, energy, and peace of mind, in the hope of becoming a top-notch surgeon. I refuse to relax and risk everything at such a crucial point in my career."
>
> "In an ambitious career there are no points which are not crucial," Nosson said. "There is never any rest. First you compete to get into a prestigious college, then the best medical school, then a good internship, a respected residency, grants, faculty positions. The thing has no end at all."
>
> "Are you working your way up to saying that my natural role in life is to be a wife and mother, and that I should give in to it gracefully? That all my father's dreams for me and all my years of work should be thrown out because I am just a girl?"
>
> "Beth," Nosson pleaded, "you cannot sacrifice your life to fulfill your father's ambitions."
>
> "These are not my father's ambitions," Beth returned hotly. "These are my own ambitions, built up through year after year of facing challenges and overcoming them."[215]

But — after knowing her father's disappointment in his own career and seeing how she was carefully inculcated from childhood with the ambition of becoming a surgeon — the reader knows better than Beth. Her ambitions are the sum of her father's disappointed ambitions to become a surgeon and to overcome discrimination against Jews and her own desire to please her father and to become a surgeon, to overcome discrimination against women. Beth has not asked herself why she has the ambition she does, what is its worth and does she truly want to fulfill it? These questions soon challenge her, begging for answers. But before she can face them, she tries to rationalize them away.

In the following excerpt, she meets an old friend from her undergraduate studies who was moderately religious and came from a religious family. She finds that he has left the Jewish fold altogether under the pressure to concentrate on his medical studies. She begins to realize that she may actually be using her own ambitions not only to please but to manipulate her parents — and herself.

> She had always felt a certain kinship for Mike, as another ambitious child of ambitious parents. For years he had used his success in school to compensate to his parents for the fact that he was gradually distancing himself from religion, just as she had, almost consciously, been compensating to her parents for the fact that she was gradually growing closer to it. Mike had gone a little too far, and the compromise had collapsed temporarily, but in the long run she supposed that he would succeed in "buying off" his parents by being "our son, the doctor." Surely a lot of children from the generation before had succeeded in making things up to their parents that way. Beth hated to think of herself as playing the same game, but she had to admit that there was a certain element of that in her behavior.
>
> After a little more consideration, she decided that it was perfectly legitimate. After all, she herself was anxious to succeed in her career, both because she had something to prove to the world about women in medicine and because she had been raised to try to excel at whatever she undertook. If it also pleased her parents and smoothed over her differences with them, so much the better. It would solve her other problem, too. If she worked herself to the point where she would need all Shabbos just to recuperate, she wouldn't have time to worry about whether or not she was lonely. That evening, the moment Shabbos was over, she resumed her studies with a single-mindedness born of near desperation.[216]

Beth completes medical school and applies for a surgical residency in the most prestigious institutions. Her chances for success are shot down by Dr. Hochberg, the renowned head of the surgical department, who decides that she should find herself a "career in some field more suited to women."[217] His reputation carries enough weight to destroy her chances, and she is emotionally crushed. However, the doctor was late in sending off his letter of "recommendation," and the next day she receives notice of her acceptance for a surgical residency in the hospital of her choice. Yet her achievement is tainted with bitterness, and her soul searching has begun in earnest. She finally takes a good look at the source of her ambitions and determines their cost to her selfhood. She concludes that to "have it all" as an ambitious career woman who wants to raise a family means compromise.

> In the old days, she would have been filled with a sort of fervent exhilaration, at the very magnitude of the challenge facing her. But now? Now the idea filled her with a profound weariness. Years of exile from the Jewish world she loved … years of unstinting labor, years of snatching prizes from others, never relaxing, never taking a vacation, because perhaps that one extra spurt of effort would tip the balance in her favor at some crucial juncture in her career.
>
> All that effort, for what? So that in the end she would claw her way back into a world where men of Dr. Hochberg's ilk were respected and powerful. A world where, no matter how high one climbs, it is never high enough, as long as there is still someone above you. And the one at the summit, is he happy? Is he secure? No…
>
> In the world of secular ambitions, there is no prize, no satisfaction that is more than momentary. Each success is but an introduction to the next struggle.…
>
> She would find a residency in a different field, here in New York, and give marriage the priority she had never allowed it to have before. The long repressed yearning to have a family to care for welled up until it almost choked her.… Though trying to be moderately successful on two fronts would never bring the accolades of outstanding success in her profession, she was not at all sure that it would not be just as challenging.[218]

A Time to Rend, a Time to Sew represents a fictional mode in ultra– Orthodox women's literature that treats the issues that we have seen throughout the literature: the embracing and adoption of Orthodox Jewish practice and the choices and changes that the heroine makes in consolidating her old ambitions with her present, chosen reality. *A Time to Rend, a Time to Sew* deals thematically with the typical *baalat teshuva's* quest: her struggle to settle questions of the self, Judaism and feminism; her unwillingness to compromise either the self or Judaism; and her repudiation or modification of what she considers Western values. *A Time to Rend, a Time to Sew* faithfully continues the convention of realism in ultra–Orthodox women's fiction.

Libby Lazewnik's novels *Between the Thorns* and *Give Me the Moon* represent a different, late-evolving strain in ultra–Orthodox contemporary fiction. The author does not deal with the women's issues we have seen in much of the personal narratives and historical fiction. The stories unfold soap opera–like, with various subplots and scenarios weaving in and out, loosely merging in the end. The characters are ordinary and well-mannered, plain, nice people for the most part. No one is overly ambitious or original, even when Lazewnik attempts to create that impression. The characters usually trod the paths that are well-worn by religious Jews. There are couples and singles. The singles seek to marry. The couples try to understand each other and improve the marriage. There is little mention of divorce, not that there has to be in a realistic ultra–Orthodox scenario. In fact, the whole social scene is perfectly realistic, with the characters each suffering disappointments and a fair share of worries.

There is also a complete acceptance of the traditional roles of women and men. In *Give Me the Moon*, for example, the focus of the two heroines, Malka and Esther, is housework. Yet this does not diminish their heroism. The field of battle of their internal and external struggles is the home. Malka's personal catharsis leads to the reaffirmation of herself despite her messy home, uneven cooking and extra pounds. Her re-empowerment manifests itself in the boldness of her matchmaking. Esther was always a compulsive house cleaner, so her personal catharsis leads her to affirm the importance of people, namely her children, over things (the house) and personal goals. The lessons these women learn in their home-bound domains are as valuable as those learned by the protagonist, Avi Weisner, a supercharismatic pulpit rabbi who lectures to large, eager audiences at his synagogue. He learns the lesson of humility, of placing individuals before his own ambitions. His lesson, in fact, is similar to that of his sister, Esther.

> "We're two of a kind, you and me," she said unexpectedly.
> He nodded. "Proud. Ambitious."

> "Perfectionists, both of us. Hard-driving and demanding the best of those around us. Determined to have things our way." She grinned wryly. "I wonder why they put up with us."
>
> "You forget one thing," he said. "We're also good choosers. We picked the right people to marry — ones who not only put up with us, but maybe even help tone us down a little."[219]

She in her sphere and he in his come to learn the same moral imperatives. In this, the author shows that self-development is not dependent on place or activity, that it is accessible to women and men even if they remain exclusively within traditional spheres of influence.

Lazewnik's *Give Me the Moon*— which does not deal with women's issues of identity, selfhood or empowerment — is also more imitative of general women's fiction. There is nothing particularly Jewish or religious about the book. For the most part, secular or even non–Jewish characters could have been plugged into the same roles and played out the same plots. Theirs are not the struggles of the *baalot teshuva* facing the conflicts between Orthodox Judaism and worldly ambitions, as in Pomerantz's *A Time to Rend, a Time to Sew* and many other novels. The characters in *Give Me the Moon* are not experiencing internal conflicts about religiosity at all. The Orthodoxy of the characters exists *de facto*. It is not a point for contemplation. Incidents that might warrant a consideration of divine will or divine intervention are discussed as if they were divorced from any spiritual destiny.

Give Me the Moon also imitates general women's fiction in that part of what keeps this book a page-turner is the reader's desire to see who will marry whom. There is a lot of courtship; of course it is in the ultra–Orthodox style of *shidduchim* (prearranged dates through a third party for the purpose of marriage), and many of the subplots end with the marriage. This tends to make the plots trite, as they focus on a brief, albeit exciting, moment in a character's life. It takes away from the realism this book attempts to generate, making it more novelistic than the other works of fiction we have discussed, more like general women's fiction.

Does Lazewnik's novel represent an attempt to achieve "normalcy" in ultra–Orthodox fiction by turning away from the theme of the *baalat teshuva*'s quest, which has already acquired the status of tired cliché? Does normalcy mean an adoption of the even more tired clichés of secular women's literature? The second option seems the more offensive, considering the unique perspective and contribution of the ultra–Orthodox woman author. Both Pomerantz's *A Time to Rend, a Time to Sew* and Lazewnik's *Give Me the Moon* were published in 1996, relatively recent additions to the still-forming genre of ultra–Orthodox fiction. It is still too early to decide which turn ultra–Orthodox fiction will take, whether or not it will move further away from its origins in the religious, woman-focused, quest-oriented personal narrative.

Fiction is the next frontier in ultra–Orthodox women's writing, fiction that does not compromise the unique message of the ultra–Orthodox woman but allows that message to be expressed in more artistically daring ways.

Notes

Introduction

1. Elaine Showalter. "Feminist Criticism in the Wilderness." In *Contemporary Literary Criticism: Literary and Cultural Studies*. Third Ed. Robert Con Davis and Ronald Schleifer. Eds. New York and London: Longman, 1994, 55. Repr. from *Critical Inquiry*. No. 8. University of Chicago Press, 1981. Also repr. in *Feminist Criticism*. Elaine Showalter. Ed. New York: Pantheon, 1985, 243–70.

2. *Ibid.*

3. *Ibid.* See also Elaine Showalter's "Toward a Feminist Poetics." In *Critical Theory since Plato*. Rev. Ed. Hazard Adams. Ed. Fort Worth, Tex.: Harcourt Brace Jovanovich, 1992, 1223–33. Repr. from *Women's Writing and Writing about Women*. Mary Jacobus. Ed. London: Croom Helm, 1979.

4. *Ibid.*, 56.

5. The essentialism of my own criticism of ultra–Orthodox women's writings will be to the extent that I will try to show the feminine independence of the authors' art. The body of work I treat is completely woman-focused. The authors themselves are women who profess the traditional Jewish tenets of a divinely granted, biologically based feminine difference. For the purposes of this study, it is helpful to remember that the organic nature and uniqueness of femininity is a *cultural* given in the ultra–Orthodox world. The admitted problems of essentialism as raised by feminist theorists will be discussed later when we focus on ultra–Orthodox claims to an essential femininity.

6. Ruth Hubbard and Marian Lowe. Eds. *Woman's Nature: Rationalizations of Inequality*. New York: Pergamon, 1984, xi, xii. See also Cynthia F. Epstein's *Deceptive Distinctions: Theory and Research on Sex, Gender and the Social Order*. New Haven, Conn.: Yale University Press, 1988, and Judith Butler's *Gender Trouble: Feminism and the Subversion of Identity*. New York: Routledge, 1989.

7. For a concise overview of the different phases in feminism and the women's movement, a helpful source is "Contemporary Feminist Theory." In Sondra Farganis. *Situating Feminism: From Thought to Action*. Thousand Oaks, Calif.: SAGE, 1994, 14–49.

8. Patrocinio Schweickart. "Reading Ourselves: Toward a Feminist Theory of Reading." In *Contemporary Literary Criticism: Literary and Cultural Studies*. Third Ed. Robert Con Davis and Ronald Schleifer. Eds. New York and London: Longman, 1994, 197.

9. *Ibid.*, 193.
10. *Ibid.*, 206.

Chapter One

11. Elizabeth V. Spelman. *Inessential Woman: Problems of Exclusion in Feminist Thought*. Boston: Beacon, 1988, 5.
12. Differing opinions on the binding nature of Jewish law is also a divisive factor among Jewish feminists, not just between feminists and traditional Jews. Feminist theologian Judith Plaskow writes:

> Discussions of halakhah easily polarize along denominational lines, with Orthodox feminists deeply concerned about the mechanisms of halakhic change and non–Orthodox feminists seeing such change either as relatively straightforward or as irrelevant. Orthodox feminists have focused their quarrels with Judaism largely on halakhic issues. Non-Orthodox feminists, myself among them, have often expressed impatience with narrowly halakhic feminist analysis. But when non–Orthodox feminists criticize Orthodox attention to halakhah, it is difficult to sort out specifically *feminist* issues from general discomfort with or lack of interest in Jewish law.

From *Standing Again at Sinai: Judaism from a Feminist Perspective*. New York: HarperCollins, 1991, 60–61.
13. Norman Lamm. "Editor's Foreword." In Moshe Meiselman. *Jewish Woman in Jewish Law*. New York: Ktav, 1978, ix.
14. *Ibid.*
15. Michael Kaufman. *Feminism and Judaism: Women, Tradition, and the Women's Movement*. Jerusalem: Heritage, 1996, xxvii–xxviii.
16. *Ibid.*, xxviii–xxix.
17. Martha Ackelsberg. "Introduction." In *Jewish Woman: New Perspectives*. Elizabeth Koltun. Ed. New York: Schocken, 1975, xiv.
18. Blu Greenberg. "Judaism and Feminism." In Koltun. Ed. *Jewish Woman: New Perspectives*, 181.
19. *Ibid.*, 185.
Greenberg here sounds like ultra–Orthodox "feminist" and scholar Tamar Frankiel, who writes:

> Jewish women certainly have the obligation to raise the issue of whether modern Western feminism honors basic Jewish values. Western culture has marginalized Jews as outsiders, and human nature, ethics, and spirituality as worthless palaver. It came as no surprise to Jewish feminists that anti–Semitism occasionally reared its head in the feminist movement as well. We should become aware that we are a non–Western (that is, not Greco-Christian) tradition, exactly as we have been treated. We must reexamine every Western thought from the perspective of our unique heritage, just as other non–Western peoples do. We must ask whether our highest values fit with those of the West, and with feminism as a response to the West. Where do we authentically stand?

From Frankiel's foreword to M. Kaufman. *Feminism and Judaism*, xix–xx.

20. Phyllis Trible. "Depatriarchalizing in Biblical Interpretation." In Koltun. Ed. *Jewish Woman: New Perspectives*, 218.

21. Judith Plaskow. "The Jewish Feminist: Conflict in Identities." In Koltun. Ed. *Jewish Woman: New Perspectives*, 3.

22. *Lilith* 15. Summer 1986, 1.

23. The *mikvah* is a pool of water that is connected to a natural water source. Immersing in the *mikvah* is an ancient Jewish practice for removing spiritual impurity. It is and has been used by both men and women for various ritualistic reasons associated with a return to a pure state. For women, the *mikvah* is most commonly associated with a return to a state where sexual relations are permitted after being forbidden during and for seven days after menstruation.

24. Elyse M. Goldstein. "Take Back the Waters: A Feminist Reappropriation of Mikvah." In *Lilith* 15. Summer 1986, 16.

25. For quick references, see Yehuda Boyar. *Kitzur Halachot beDinei Niddah*. In Hebrew. Bnai Brak: Yehuda Boyar, 1982, 50; S. Wagschal. *Taharas Am Yisroel*. In English. Jerusalem: Feldheim, 1982, 33; and Shlomo Ganzfried. *Kitzur Shulchon Oruch*. Vol. 2. Trans. and annotated by Eliyahu Touger. New York and Jerusalem: Moznaim, 1991, 657.

The *Kitzur Shulchon Oruch* implies that some sort of additional modesty is in order while saying the blessing in the water, such as making the water cloudy before saying the blessing in the case where the *mikvah* has a mud floor (which is unheard-of nowadays). But, even here, there is no mention of covering breasts.

26. Goldstein. "Take Back the Waters," 16.

27. Plaskow. *Standing Again at Sinai*, 240.

28. Michael Kaufman. *Feminism and Judaism*, 314.

29. Hillel Halkin. "Feminizing Jewish Studies." In *Commentary*. February 1998, 41.

30. *Ibid.*, 43.

31. *Ibid.*, 44.

32. Linda Grant. "The Supermarket of Gender Politics: Men v. Women in the 1990s." In *The Jewish Quarterly*. Spring 1997, 6.

33. *Ibid.*, 7.

34. Michelene Wandor. "The Sex Divide in Jewish Culture: A Meditation on Jewishness and Gender." In *The Jewish Quarterly*. Spring 1997, 13.

35. Grant. "The Supermarket of Gender Politics," 7.

36. *Ibid.*

37. Elizabeth Powers. "A Farewell to Feminism." In *Commentary*. January 1997.

38. For example, see Judith Hauptman's *Rereading the Rabbis: A Woman's Voice*. Boulder, Colo.: Westview, 1998. See also Micah D. Halpern, and Chana Safrai. Eds. *Jewish Legal Writings by Women*. Jerusalem: Urim, 1998; and Joel B. Wolowelsky, *Women, Jewish Law, and Modernity: New Opportunitites in a Post-Feminist Age*. Hoboken, N.J.: Ktav, 1997.

39. Nelly Furman. "Textual Feminism." In *Women and Language in Literature and Society*. Ruth Borker, Sally McConnell-Ginet and Nelly Furman. Eds. New York: Praeger, 1980, 51.

40. *Ibid.*, 52.

41. Ferdinand de Saussure. "Nature of the Linguistic Sign." From *Course in General Linguistics.* Trans. Wade Baskins. Repr. in *Critical Theory since Plato.* Rev. Ed. Hazard Adams. Ed. Fort Worth, Tex.: Harcourt Brace Jovanovich, 1992, 718–26.

Chapter Two

42. Debra Renee Kaufman. *Rachel's Daughters: Newly Orthodox Jewish Women.* New Brunswick and London: Rutgers University Press, 1991, 113–114. See also Lynn Davidman. *Tradition in a Rootless World: Women Turn to Orthodox Judaism.* Berkeley, Calif.: University of California Press, 1991, 117–118.

43. D. Kaufman. *Rachel's Daughters*, x.

44. *Ibid.*, 132–33.

45. *Ibid.*, 155.

46. Butler. *Gender Trouble*, 4.

47. Judith Hauptman writes, "I am troubled by the contemporary assumption that the presence of patriarchy necessarily precludes the possibility of those within it acting on women's behalf.... It is also possible to conclude that absolute patriarchy is only a theoretical projection, a construct, not a reality.... Recent research in the Bible and my own evaluation of the Talmud suggest that rabbinic society is more accurately characterized as a 'benevolent patriarchy.'" In *Rereading the Rabbis*, 5.

48. *Ibid.*, 165–66.

49. *Ibid.*, 166.

50. Tamar El-Or. *Educated and Ignorant: Ultraorthodox Jewish Women and Their World.* Trans. Haim Watzman. Boulder, Colo. and London: Lynne Rienner, 1994.

51. *Ibid.*, 65.

52. That Judaism requires only married women to cover their hair leads to the conclusion that the hair covering is not only for reasons of modesty. If it were, unmarried women would also be required to cover their hair, just as they practice all other conventions of modest dress and behavior. Or, there might be a more ethereal, unapparent immodesty associated with the uncovered hair of only a married woman.

53. A personal experience reinforces this evaluation. I am reminded of an incident that illustrates the maximalistic approach to Jewish observance that marks ultra–Orthodox Jews. I was invited to be the guest of a strictly observant family in Jerusalem during Sukkot, an eight-day festival that includes the building of, sleeping in and eating in temporary dwellings. The roof of the *sukkah* must be situated under the open sky in order to be valid. As a positive, time-bound *mitzvah*, women are exempt from dwelling in the *sukkah*. The eldest daughter of my host was leaning back in her chair, which placed her head under the part of the *sukkah*'s roof that was not under the open sky, thus at that moment she was not fulfilling the *mitzvah* of *sukkah*. Her father pointed out that she should move forward since she was not in the *sukkah*, to which the girl replied, "So what? Women are exempt from dwelling in the *sukkah*." The look of consternation on her father's face was enough for the girl to see that her attitude was unacceptable.

54. Sarah Shapiro gives an example of the questions that a Jewish mother faces when she diverts her attention from her home caring in order to not learn Torah, in this case, but to write. For her, writing is also an activity of importance, a source of happiness and a way to get in touch with her nature and the divine power that gave her such a nature. Writing, as a pursuit that is artistic for her and outside the realm of religious obligations, is more debatable than learning Torah. She asks, "Could I in good conscience take time out from parenting and homemaking — the value of which was beyond question from a religious standpoint — for such a self-centered activity as writing?" She questions if artistic endeavors are a "legitimate way to serve God," especially when they include personal ambitions.

See Shapiro's "On Jewish Mothers and Their Writing." In *Don't You Know It's a Perfect World?* Southfield, Mich.: Targum, 1998, 52–53.

55. The *mitzvah* (Torah obligation) of raising children does not completely explain women's exemption from the *mitzvah* of Torah study, or otherwise women who were not occupied with raising children would not be exempt from study as a general rule. Some sources indicate that women's intellectual makeup has to do with women historically being discouraged from studying (actually, being taught) certain parts of the Torah. Many contemporary authorities hold that what was applicable in a former age does not apply today in an age when women are used to being taught and are expected to study. This is based on the Rambam's qualification of teaching women in the Middle Ages for the reason that they themselves were not interested in vigorous study, which is considered an outdated reason. In either case, in the contemporary version of a maximalistic orientation toward practice, women's study has become a social imperative despite the fact that they are not halakhically required to study as men are.

Other sources indicate that women do not need Torah study to be obligatory because they do not need the *tikkun* (spiritual rectification) inherent in the performance of this *mitzvah* or any *mitzvah* from which they are exempt. This is based on the understanding that Torah obligations serve to perfect the one who performs them. This implies that women are ontologically on a higher spiritual level and need not be obligated to study.

Whether the exemption is based on women's homemaking priorities, intellectual capacities or spiritual makeup, Jewish sources say that the observance of a *mitzvah*, even one that is done voluntarily, earns reward.

For an in-depth discussion of women's obligations, exemptions and practices in fulfilling Torah commandments, including studying Torah in the past and today, refer to Michael Kaufman's *The Woman in Jewish Law and Tradition*. Northvale, N.J. and London: Jason Aronson, 1993. An especially thorough treatment of the issue of women's Torah study is Shoshana Pantel Zolty's *"And All Your Children Shall Be Learned": Women and the Study of Torah in Jewish Law and History*. Northvale, N.J.: Jason Aronson, 1993.

56. Tamar El-Or. "Power/Knowledge/Gender: The Oranges-and-Grapefruit Debate." In *Judaism since Gender*. Miriam Peskowitz and Laura Levitt. Eds. New York: Routledge, 1997, 64.

57. *Ibid.*, 65.

58. *Ibid.*

Chapter Three

59. The religious/cultural response, like the literary one, has been to strengthen Orthodox "feminism" from within, to bolster a feeling of women's empowerment from traditional sources. Orthodox Jewish leaders have responded to Jewish feminism but, again, not directly to the source of intimidation. Directives to counteract Jewish feminism address the religious population itself. Michael Kaufman gives a particularly severe example of how religious leaders perceive and sometimes respond to feminism:

> Dancing with the Torah scrolls is an activity that has traditionally been done by men. Under the influence of the women's movement there has in recent years been an effort in some traditional synagogues on the part of some women to conduct *hakafot* [circle dancing] with the Torah scrolls on Simhat Torah. While a woman, like a man, is permitted to touch and hold the Torah scroll at all times, the practice of women's *hakafot* has been opposed by all contemporary halachic authorities.
>
> Rabbinic opposition to women's *hakafot* is apparently based not on *Halacha*, but simply because the practice is viewed as an innovation in traditional practice that is advocated by a movement they see as undermining Judaism. Many traditional rabbinic leaders view feminism as linked to antifamilism and the destruction of the Jewish family in America in the last decades, and therefore a movement antagonistic to Jewish continuity — an implacable foe to be firmly resisted. Consequently, these authorities oppose all innovations in traditional Jewish practice that are influenced by feminism.

In *The Woman in Jewish Law and Tradition*, 222.

60. Rachel Adler. "The Jew Who Wasn't There: *Halakha* and the Jewish Woman." In *Davka*. Summer 1971.

61. Yisroel Miller. *In Search of the Jewish Woman: A Torah Journey*. Jerusalem: Feldheim, 1984, 72–73.

62. Zolty. *"And All Your Children Shall Be Learned,"* 40.

63. B. Davids. Photography by Allen Shumeister. "A New Generation: Women Returning to Judaism." In *Wellsprings: A Quarterly Journal Exploring the Inner Dimensions of Torah and Jewish Life*. Fall 1990, 22–25.

64. Tzivia Emmer. "Sanctity and Self: Conversations with Chabad Women." In *Wellsprings*. Fall 1993, 15–29.

65. *Ibid.*, 13.

66. Jack Kugelmass. "Jewish Icons: Envisioning the Self in Images of the Other." In *Jews and Other Differences: The New Jewish Cultural Studies*. Jonathan Boyarin and Daniel Boyarin. Eds. Minneapolis and London: University of Minnesota Press, 1997, 30–53.

67. Miriam Grossman. "Antidote for the Existential Blues." In *Aura: A Reader on Jewish Womanhood*. Tema Gurary. Ed. New York: Lubavitch Women's Organization, 1984, 5.

68. Rabbi Heschel Greenberg. "Mitzvos as Purification." Gurary. Ed. In *Aura*. 51–55.

69. *Ibid.*

70. Michael Kaufman puts forth the same argument based on some of the same Torah authorities and many different ones. He comes to Greenberg's conclusion that men perform "unconditional" positive commandments "in order to attain a level of spirituality that women by their nature already enjoy"(*The Woman in Jewish Law and Tradition*, 210).

Greenberg explains that the three positive commandments that are traditionally performed by women qualitatively make up for the reduced number of positive commandments encumbent upon them. Kaufman's argument, however, focuses on putting the halakhic phenomenon into proportion:

> Of the 248 Positive Commandments in Maimonides' enumeration of the Torah's 613 *mitzvot* [commandments], the *Rambam* finds that 60 are incumbent on every adult Jew at all times and at all places and under all circumstances. Maimonides notes: "Of these 'Unconditional Commandments,' 46 are binding upon women as well as men, and 14 are not binding upon women"(Maimonides, *Sefer HaMitzvot*, Positive Commandments, end)....
>
> There is no differentiation between men and women in their obligations to observe the 365 Negative Precepts of the Torah.
>
> The reasons that certain [14] *mitzvot* are incumbent on men and not on women are varied: certain *mitzvot* cannot be performed by women simply because of physical inapplicability — for example, causing one's wife to rejoice during the first year of marriage, circumcision, not cutting off the peyot at the sides of the beard....
>
> Similarly, the exemption of women from the *mitzvot* of marrying and having children are based on Judaism's sensitivity to the physical hazards of pregnancy and childbirth for the woman (R. Meir Simha of Dvinsk, *Meshech Hochma, Parashat Noah, Peru*) Therefore, these are elective *mitzvot* for women that they can optionally accept upon themselves.

From M. Kaufman. *The Woman in Jewish Law and Tradition*, 207–8. See also Samson Raphael Hirsch. *Commentary on Leviticus* 23:43. Vol. 3 of *The Pentateuch: Commentary on the Torah*. Trans. Isaac Levy. London: Judaica Press, 1989. For a discussion of the spectrum of explanations for women's exemption and their practical effect, see Zolty. *"And All Your Children Shall Be Learned,"* 41–47. See also Meiselman. *Jewish Woman in Jewish Law*, 43–48.

71. Susan A. Handelman. (Shaina Sarah). "Niddah and Mikvah — A Chasidic Approach." In Gurary. Ed. *Aura*. 59.

72. S. Feldbrand. *From Sarah to Sarah*. Brooklyn, N.Y.: Feldbrand, Key-Tov Graphics and Moriah Offset, 1980.

73. Sondra Henry and Emily Taitz. *Written Out of History: Our Jewish Foremothers*. Fourth ed. New York: Biblio Press, 1990.

74. Menachem M. Brayer. *The Jewish Woman in Rabbinic Literature: A Psychosocial Perspective*. Vol. 1. Hoboken, N.J.: Ktav, 1986, xiii.

75. Henry and Taitz. *Written Out of History*, 66–67.

76. *Ibid.*, 67.

77. *Ibid.*

Chapter Four

78. Tamar Frankiel. *The Voice of Sarah: Feminine Spirituality and Traditional Judaism*. San Francisco: HarperCollins, 1990, 2.

79. *Ibid.*, xiv.

80. The idea of rereading history is not original. Feminists in the field of psychology have advocated just such an activity for recovering feminine heroines or archetypes unencumbered by patriarchal social contexts. They usually reread primitive myths, and their conclusions are very different from those of Frankiel. See, for example, Nor Hall. *The Moon and the Virgin: Reflections on the Archetypal Feminine*. New York: Harper and Row, 1980; Sylvia Brinton Perera. *Descent to the Goddess: A Way of Initiation for Women*. Toronto: Inner City Books, 1981; and Meredith A. Powers. *The Heroine in Western Literature: The Archetype and Her Reemergence in Modern Prose*. Jefferson, N.C. and London: McFarland, 1991.

81. Frankiel. *The Voice of Sarah*, 43.

82. *Ibid.*, 42.

83. *Ibid.*, 48.

84. *Ibid.*, 48–49.

85. *Ibid.*, 2.

86. *Ibid.*, 113–14.

87. M. Kaufman. *The Woman in Jewish Law and Tradition*, xxii.

88. *Ibid.*, xxvi.

89. *Ibid.*, xxvii.

90. *Ibid.*, xxix.

91. *Ibid.*, xxi.

92. *Ibid.*, xxxiii. Kaufman reiterates the importance of Jewish education in *Feminism and Judaism*, where he explains how poor Jewish education led to an undiscriminating acceptance of foreign (feminist) values:

> Thus, the process of cultural assimilation ... is helped further along by the erosion of the intellectual underpinnings of Jewish practice. Without the knowledge of how to live Jewishly, without the intellectual *raison d'etre*, Judaism may begin to seem archaic, unrelated to the pressing realities of people's daily lives. Where were the teachers, the elders, the wise — those who could have explained how the Jewish tradition was totally relevant? Ultimately, the disruption of the educational process results in the death of the religious practice.

From M. Kaufman. *Feminism and Judaism*, xxv.

Many other defenders of Jewish tradition reiterate that ignorance of Judaism is a primary factor in its being rejected. For example, Moshe Meiselman writes:

> The modern Jewish woman, educated with all the sophistication of twentieth-century culture, finds herself in the awkward position of being more conversant with alien cultures than with her own. To have a sophisticated view of everything else and a Sunday School knowledge of Judaism is an unforgivable crime. It is of utmost importance that women deepen their knowledge of their Jewish heritage from a specifically Jewish perspective.

In Moshe Meiselman. *Jewish Woman in Jewish Law*, 173.

Shoshana Pantel Zolty writes that Jewish education will enlighten women as to their true, esteemed status in Jewish tradition:

> What often troubles some women are actually insensitive actions or remarks that are foreign to authentic Jewish tradition. This is one reason why a sound Jewish education is so vital; all Jewish men and women need to be educated as to the equal value of women and men in the eyes of God.

From Zolty. *"And All Your Children Shall Be Learned,"* 40.

93. M. Kaufman. *The Woman in Jewish Law and Tradition*, xxxiv.

94. Lisa Aiken. *To Be a Jewish Woman*. Northvale, N.J.: Jason Aronson, 1992, xxi–xxii.

95. *Ibid.*, xxiii.

96. *Ibid.*, 31.

97. *Ibid.*, 194.

98. *Ibid.*

99. Betty Friedan. *The Feminine Mystique*. New York: Norton, 1973.

100. Susan Weidman Schneider. Ed. *Jewish and Female*. New York: Simon and Schuster, 1985, 22.

101. M. Kaufman. *Feminism and Judaism*, 316.

102. *Ibid.*, 314.

103. *Ibid.*, 314–15.

104. *Ibid.*, xxvii.

105. *Ibid.*, 314.

106. *Ibid.*, 65.

107. Suzanne Gordon. *Prisoner of Men's Dreams*. Boston: Little, Brown, 1991, 8.

108. The following quote from a nineteenth-century work that draws on *kabbalah* [esoteric Jewish scholarship] explains how "masculine" and "feminine" are concepts that have far-reaching, cosmic significance in Jewish thought.

> All the worlds and all creations are represented as masculine and feminine, that is, as influential and receptive, because the world that is higher influences the world that is lower…. But, in the future [final redemption], everyone will rectify his portion of soul to its root, and the sparks of holiness will rise, and the external forces will be completely nullified. Then the light of clarity of godliness will appear in all the worlds. And the circle and the line will be equal. [The line represents the current dominant mode of hierarchical influence. The circle represents the future, preferred mode of equal influence; every part of the circle being equidistant from its center.] And then there will not be masculine and feminine aspects, because everyone will equally perceive the light of God, blessed is His name.

From Rabbi Klonymus Kalmen Halevy Epstein's *Meor v'Shemesh*. (Free translation from the Hebrew). On Torah verse in *Shemot, parashat Beshalach* 15:20. 1842. I thank Devora Fastag for pointing out this source in her unpublished essay "The Secret of *Nekevah Tesovev Gever*." Jerusalem, 1997.

This excerpt implies that in Jewish thought 1) "masculinity" and "femininity" are envisioned as modes of existential being. This implies much more than the common usage of these terms as attributes associated with the male and female;

2) Any issue of inequality between these modes has to do with the ability to directly perceive and emit divine effluence — in masculinity as influential and femininity as receptive (this is very different from feminist challenges of inequality, which are based on the access to public, social power); and 3) Even this ontological inequality demands rectification, whereby the clarity of godlinesss is perceived equally by all directly from its source.

109. M. Kaufman. *Feminism and Judaism*, xxx.

110. Zolty. *"And All Your Children Shall Be Learned,"* 26.

Chapter Five

111. Josephine Donovan. "The Silence Is Broken." In Borker et al. Eds. *Women and Language in Literature and Society*, 212.

112. *Ibid.*, 213.

113. From discussion with Chaya Rivka Jessel, a religious writer, and supported by other critics.

114. "Introduction to Part Four." In Borker et al. Eds. *Women and Language in Literature and Society*, 219.

115. Michel Beaujour. *Poetics of the Literary Self-Portrait*. Trans. Yara Milos. New York and London: New York University Press, 1991, 4–5.

116. *Ibid.*, 9.

117. *Ibid.*, 10.

118. Mary G. Mason. "The Other Voice: Autobiographies of Women Writers." In *Life/Lines: Theorizing Women's Autobiography*. Bella Brodzki and Celeste Schenck. Eds. Ithaca, N.Y., and London: Cornell University Press, 1988, 22.

119. *Ibid.*, 44.

120. Carolyn G. Heilbrun. *Writing a Woman's Life*. New York and London: W.W. Norton, 1988, 16.

121. *Ibid.*, 18.

122. Mason. "The Other Voice: Autobiographies of Women Writers," 22.

123. *Ibid.*

Chapter Six

124. Sarah Shapiro. *Growing with My Children*. Southfield, Mich.: Targum, 1990, 347–48.

125. Shapiro. *Don't You Know It's a Perfect World?*, 133.

126. *Ibid.*, 136–37.

127. *Ibid.*, 87–89.

128. *Ibid.*, 97.

129. *Ibid.*, 192.

130. *Ibid.*, 15–16.

131. In a different passage, Shapiro also makes a connection between darkness, really dark hair, Jewishness and otherness: "My hair was dark, too (in our

non–Jewish, blonde town)." In *Don't You Know It's a Perfect World?*, 65–66. Marge Piercy's heroine in *He, She and It* also feels "too Jewish, too dark" (New York: Fawcett Crest, 1991, 5).

132. Spelman. *Inessential Woman*, 58.

133. Shapiro writes, "I'd skimmed through *The Feminine Mystique* — one of my other sisters had brought it home from college — and knew male chauvinism when I saw it. My mother was coddling her husband, as usual.... I was disgusted by my mother for letting herself be used." From *Don't You Know It's a Perfect World?*, 23–24.

134. Yaffa Ganz. *All things Considered ... From a Woman's Point of View ....* New York: Mesorah, 1990, 15–16.

135. Yaffa Ganz. *Cinnamon and Myrrh.* Jerusalem: Feldheim, 1994, 109–10.

136. Mindy Gross. *How Long the Night.* Southfield, Mich.: Targum, 1991, 29.

137. *Ibid.*, 31–32.

138. *Ibid.*, 33–34.

139. *Ibid.*, 85–86.

140. Mason. "The Other Voice: Autobiographies of Women Writers," 44.

141. Brodzki and Schenck. Eds. *Life/Lines*, 2.

Chapter Seven

142. Ganz. *Cinnamon and Myrrh*, 110.

143. Sarah Shapiro. Ed. *Of Home and Heart: Reflections on the World of the Jewish Woman.* New York: Mesorah, 1993, 15.

144. Bread eaten on the Sabbath, often home-baked. It is usually braided and covered with poppy or sesame seeds.

145. "Holy Sabbath, Holy Sabbath."

146. Bracha Druss Goetz. "Between the Braids." In Shapiro. Ed. *Of Home and Heart*, 47–48.

147. Sheina Medwed humorously points out her own integration dilemma in terms of her increasing "body awareness":

> Now I was caught in a very confusing bind. On the one hand, I had my feminist training against media images of women. I had stopped watching television and reading women's magazines for quite a while. Now I was confronted with Judaism's ideal of the woman, and a very attractive one at that. I couldn't walk into Orthodoxy in my overalls and hiking boots.

From "Making Peace with My Body." In Sarah Shapiro. Ed. *More of Our Lives: An Anthology of Jewish Women's Writings.* Southfield, Mich.: Targum, 1993, 378.

148. Bracha Druss Goetz. "Wonder Woman." In Shapiro. Ed. *Of Home and Heart*, 156.

149. Alicia Ostriker. "The Nerves of a Midwife: Contemporary American Women's Poetry." From *Parnassus: Poetry in Review.* In *The Pushcart Prize IV: Best of the Small Presses.* Bill Henderson. Ed. New York: Avon, 1979, 468.

150. Varda Branfman. "Bread." In Sarah Shapiro. Ed. *Our Lives: An Anthology of Jewish Women's Writings.* Southfield, Mich.: Targum, 1991, 135–36.

151. The connection between the bread metaphor and women has a firm basis in Judaism. The Torah states that Potiphar appointed Joseph ruler over his estate and affairs and trusted him so completely that he "left everything he had in Joseph's hand, and did not concern himself with anything other than the bread that he ate" (Genesis 39:6). Rashi comments that "bread" in this verse is a metaphor for Potiphar's wife.

Rabbi Matityahu Glazerson explains that the use of bread as a metaphor for woman describes her capacity to complete her husband's person. Bread in Hebrew is *lekhem*, from the root meaning to join or weld together, *l'halkhim*. Bread keeps together the two foundations of a human being, body and soul, just as a woman joins together with her husband in faithful union and keeps his spiritual and material worlds together. As the Gemara states, "A man should always be careful of his wife's honor for blessing is found in a man's home for her sake" (*Bava Metzia* 59a). A husband is granted material plenitude in his wife's merit. Their faithfulness to each other is associated with economic well-being in their home. From Glazerson's *The Secret in the Foundation of Marriage*. In Hebrew, *Hasod Shebayesod Hanisuin*. Jerusalem: Meor Hagalil, 1986.

152. In Shapiro. Ed. *More of Our Lives*, xvii.

153. *Ibid.*, xxiv.

154. I thank Chaya Rivkah Jessel for pointing out the prevalence of the mother as a point of reference in ultra–Orthodox women's writings.

155. See, for example, Shoshana Lepon's "A Shabbos in the Hospital," where the author hears the "woman in the pink robe" tell the postpartum mothers:

> "If you already have a family at home, having another baby presents a new challenge. You don't need this baby to make you a mother. You don't need him to give you purpose in life.
>
> "Not only do you have children at home, you may even have *little* children. There may have been no pressing *need* for this baby — at least not right now. But that is exactly the point. Our first few children answer *our* needs; we appreciate them for themselves, but also for what they give *us*. Then Hashem blesses us with children even after we feel fulfilled. We are given this opportunity to bring Jewish souls into the world not for our own sake but for *His*."

In Shapiro. Ed. *More of Our Lives*, 207.

156. See Miriam Adahan's "The Seventh Candle, Which Will Forever Remain Unlit." In Shapiro. Ed. *More of Our Lives*, 151–57.

157. Anonymous. "To Rock in the Sun." In Shapiro. Ed. *More of Our Lives*, 125.

158. Gillah Amoch. "Dearest Mummy." In Shapiro. Ed. *More of Our Lives*, 219–24.

159. Felicity Amoch. "Blossoms." In Shapiro. Ed. *More of Our Lives*, 225–30.

160. Joanne Jackson Yelenik. "A Balabusta Coming Full Circle." In Shapiro. Ed. *More of Our Lives*, 423.

161. *Ibid.*, 422.

162. Chana Siegel. "My Mother's Sewing Room." In Shapiro. Ed. *More of Our Lives*, 354.

163. Chaya Rivkah Jessel. "My Mother's Garden." In Shapiro. Ed. *More of Our Lives*, 242, 243.

164. Chana Siegel. "My Mother's Sewing Room." In Shapiro. Ed. *More of Our Lives*, 355.

165. Jessel. "My Mother's Garden." In Shapiro. Ed. *More of Our Lives*, 243.

166. Shapiro. *Don't You Know It's a Perfect World?*, 178.

Chapter Eight

167. Pearl Benisch. *To Vanquish the Dragon*. Jerusalem: Feldheim, 1991, vii–viii.

168. Rabbi Joseph Telushkin writes, "Younger Israelis had a more complicated response [to the Eichmann trial in 1960]. Many were ashamed to learn that most Jews had not fought back against the Nazis, and unfavorably contrasted their behavior with that of the Israeli Army. The expression 'They went like sheep to the slaughter' (a reworking of Psalms 44:23) was applied to the six million derogatorily."

From *Jewish Literacy*. New York: William Morrow, 1991, 375.

169. Anna Eilenberg. *Sisters in the Storm*. Lakewood, N.J.: CIS, 1992, 192–93.

170. Traditionally, Jewish women light at least two candles before the onset of the Sabbath. Two candles are symbolic of the two expressions used in the biblical injunctions to keep the Sabbath, *zachor* and *shamor*, which literally mean remember and guard, respectively (Exodus 20:8 and Deuteronomy 5:12).

171. Benisch. *To Vanquish the Dragon*. 311–12.

172. *Ibid.*, 160–61.

173. *Ibid.*, 164–65.

174. Joan Ringelheim writes that the tendency to understate or ignore sex-related issues in the Holocaust is certainly understandable. No one wants to deal with the unpalatable possibility that female family members and friends may have been raped or may have used sex to buy food or security. Ringelheim claims that sex as a "delicate and intimate" issue makes it difficult as a subject of Holocaust research. But it is this very difficulty in dealing with an issue that is so specific to women, she argues, that hinders our ability to understand women's victimization in the Holocaust. Ringelheim writes that "women's lives are ignored and/or forgotten" among the arguments that sexual exploitation, rape, pregnancy and abortion may be specific to women's experience in general but are not Holocaust-specific, or that talking about sexuality in women's victimization represents a desecration of their memories. From "Gender and Genocide: A Split Memory." A paper prepared for presentation at the Conference on Women in the Holocaust in Jerusalem, June 19–22, 1995.

175. "Despite [the targeting and destruction of women], relatively little attention has been paid to women's experiences before, during, and after the Holocaust. Much of the best witness literature by women, the autobiographical accounts of those who survived the Holocaust, is out of print or not easily accessible. Much of the most widely read scholarship — historical, sociopolitical, philosophical, and religious — treats the Holocaust as if sexual and gender differences did not make

a difference. A lot of significant detail has gone unmentioned if not unnoticed. Thus the particularities of women's experiences and reflections have been submerged and ignored." From the preface to Carol Rittner and John K. Roth. Eds. *Different Voices: Women and the Holocaust*. New York: Paragon, 1993, xi.

176. See Rittner and Roth. Eds. *Different Voices*. An example at hand is Aranka Siegal's autobiographical account, told by "Piri," who, during her recovery in a hospital just after liberation, recalls "Mindi's pleading and fighting with the doctors for an abortion. 'I'm not taking an SS bastard child home with me,' she had shouted one day. 'I'm only twenty. I want to start a new life.' Her sisters tried to quiet her in their embarrassment. 'Who did I do it for, if not to save you from starvation? This is the thanks I get. Suddenly you can afford the luxury of shame.'" From Aranka Siegal's *Grace in the Wilderness: After the Liberation 1945–1948*. New York: Farrar Strauss Giroux, 1985, 16.

177. Alvin H. Rosenfeld. *A Double Dying: Reflections on Holocaust Literature*. Bloomington and London: Indiana University Press, 1980, 164.

178. Benisch. *To Vanquish the Dragon*, 256–58.

179. R.L. Klein. *The Scent of Snowflowers*. Jerusalem: Feldheim, 1989, 189.

180. *Ibid.*, 495.

181. Together these Hebrew phrases make up a biblical verse (Deuteronomy 6:4) that is usually translated as "Hear, O Israel, the Lord [is] our G-d, the Lord is one." Rabbi Joseph Telushkin writes that this verse, known as the *Sh'ma*,

> comes closest to being Judaism's credo. In just six Hebrew words, it sums up Judaism's belief in monotheism, and its rejection of all idols. For two thousand years, the *Sh'ma* has been the verse with which many Jewish martyrs have gone to their deaths, while those fortunate enough to meet more peaceful endings try to die with the *Sh'ma* on their lips. To this day, Jews are supposed to recite the *Sh'ma* four times a day, twice during morning prayers, once during the evening service, and, finally, at home before going to sleep.

From Telushkin. *Jewish Literacy*, 667.

182. Klein. *The Scent of Snowflowers*, 509.

183. *Ibid.*, 101.

184. *Ibid.*, 101, 102.

185. Beaujour. *Poetics of the Literary Self-Portrait*, 9–10.

186. Myrna Goldenberg. "Holocaust Literature: The Burden of Gender." A paper prepared in June 1995 (unpublished).

In a different place, she writes, "Many female survivors believe that their training and experiences as traditional housekeepers and family care-givers contributed to their survival." From "Testimony, Narrative, and Nightmare." In Maurie Sacks. Ed. *Active Voices: Women in Jewish Culture*. Urbana and Chicago, Ill.: University of Illinois Press, 1995, 100. See also Sybil Milton in Rittner and Roth. Eds. *Different Voices*, 227–32, and Joan Ringelheim in Rittner and Roth. Eds. *Different Voices*, 380–84.

187. Eilenberg. *Sisters in the Storm*, 144–45.

188. An exception is Peska Friedman's *Going Forward*, in which she hints at the moral and spiritual degeneration among Jews even during the early part of the Holocaust (New York: Mesorah, 1994).

189. Mussia Deiches. "A Bittersweet Laughter." In Jehoshua Eibeshitz and

Anna Eilenberg-Eibeshitz. Eds. and Trans. *Women in the Holocaust: A Collection of Testimonies*. Vol. 2. New York: Remember, 1994, 178–79.

Chapter Nine

190. Literally, "helper opposite him," from Genesis 2:18.
191. Sarah Chana Radcliffe. *Aizer K'negdo: The Jewish Woman's Guide to Happiness in Marriage*. Southfield, Mich.: Targum, 1988, 19.
192. Miriam Adahan. *It's All a Gift*. Jerusalem: Feldheim, 1992, 93–94.
193. Miriam Adahan. "Feeling Worthwhile — With or without a Man." In *The Miriam Adahan Handbook: "Nobody's Perfect": Maintaining Emotional Health*. Southfield, Mich.: Targum, 1994, 42.
194. *Ibid.*, 48.
195. *Ibid.*, 41.
196. *Ibid.*, 48.
197. *Bat Kol: Jewish Women's Journal*. No. 5. Rivkah Shifren. Ed. Jerusalem, 1996. (Vol. 1, No. 1 published in Los Angeles, 1994.)
198. I refer to Sandra M. Gilbert and Susan Gubar's use of the phrase in *The Madwoman in the Attic*. New Haven and London: Yale University Press, 1979.

Chapter Ten

199. This opinion was voiced in an unusually outspoken article: Chana Siegel's "Where Have All the Writers Gone?: In Search of Jewish Fiction." In *Bat Kol: Jewish Women's Journal*. No. 5, 1996, 3–4.
200. I thank Sara Gergel for suggesting this idea.
201. I thank Chaya Rivkah Jessel for bringing Piercy's novel to my attention, and for lending me her copy.
202. Shoshana Lepon. *No Greater Treasure: Stories of Extraordinary Women Drawn from the Talmud and Midrash*. Southfield, Mich.: Targum, 1990; and *And Rachel Was His Wife*. Marsi Tabak. Ed. Jerusalem: Feldheim, 1990.
203. Rosalie Lamet. *City of Diamonds*. Southfield, Mich.: Targum, 1996, 165.
204. *Ibid.*, 306.
205. See Goldenberg. "Testimony, Narrative, and Nightmare." In Sacks. Ed. *Active Voices*, 102.
206. Dvora Waysman. *The Pomegranate Pendant: A Historical Novel*. Jerusalem: Feldheim, 1995, 91.
207. Susan Sniader Lanser. *Fictions of Authority: Women Writers and Narrative Voice*. Ithaca, N.Y. and London: Cornell University Press, 1992, 17–18.
208. Talmud. *Berachot* 17a.
209. Talmud. *Bava Batra* 9a.
210. M. Kaufman. *The Woman in Jewish Law and Tradition*, 38.
211. *And Rachel Was His Wife*, 71.

212. Talmud. *Ketubot* 63a; *Nedarim* 50a.

213. Frankiel. *The Voice of Sarah*, 2.

214. Rachel Pomerantz. *A Time to Rend, a Time to Sew.* Jerusalem: Feldheim, 1996, 55–56.

215. *Ibid.*, 132–33.

216. *Ibid.*, 151–52.

217. *Ibid.*, 213.

218. *Ibid.*, 215–16.

219. Libby Lazewnik. *Give Me the Moon.* Southfield, Mich.: Targum, 1996, 414.

Bibliography

Nonfiction

AUTOBIOGRAPHIES/BIOGRAPHIES

Abramson, Chaya Malka. As told to Esther Tscholkowsky. *Who by Fire: The True Story of a Young Mother's Faith and Courage, and the Compassionate Community That Helped Bring about Her Miraculous Recovery.* Jerusalem: Feldheim, 1995.

Bald, Gittel Birnhack. *Timeless Tripod.* New York: Tamar, 1993.

Bat-Am, Devora. *A Song of Ascent: A Jewish Woman's Search.* Southfield, Mich.: Targum, 1992.

Dansky, Miriam. *Rebbetzin Grunfeld: The Life of Judith Grunfeld, Courageous Pioneer of the Bais Yaakov Movement and Jewish Rebirth.* New York: Mesorah, 1994.

_____. *Reflections: A Collection of Poetry and Prose.* Southfield, Mich.: Targum, 1991.

Ganz, Yaffa. *All things Considered ... From a Woman's Point of View....* New York: Mesorah, 1990.

_____. *Cinnamon and Myrrh.* Jerusalem: Feldheim, 1994.

Gold, Yeshara. *I Lift My Eyes: True Stories of Spiritual Triumph.* Southfield, Mich.: Targum, 1990.

Gottlieb, Anna. *In Between the Lines: A Collection of Memories, Discoveries, Observations, Hopes, Dreams, Realities and Other Little Pieces of Life.* Princeton, N.J.: Bristol, Rhein and Englander, 1992.

Greenberg, Rebbetzin Esther. *Woman to Woman.* Aviva Rappaport. Ed. New York: Mesorah, 1996.

Greenhut, Gitel. *Mamuka: A Memoir.* Lakewood, N.J.: CIS, 1991.

Gross, Mindy. *How Long the Night.* Southfield, Mich.: Targum, 1991.

Horowitz, Raichel. *The Bostoner Rebbetzin Remembers.* New York: Mesorah, 1996.

Krohn, Hindy. *The Way It Was: Touching Vignettes about Growing Up Jewish in the Philadelphia of Long Ago.* New York: Mesorah, 1989.

Mantel, Chana. *Lidingo: Memories of the Small Swedish Haven Which 120 Girls Called Home After the Holocaust.* Jerusalem: Machon Yachdav, 1998.

Mordechai, Tova. *Playing with Fire: One Woman's Remarkable Odyssey.* New York: BP, 1991.

Rosengarten, Sudy. *Worlds Apart: The Birth of Bais Yaakov in America: A Personal Recollection.* Southfield, Mich.: Targum, 1992.

Samsonowitz, Miriam. *Grandma: Mrs. Devorah Sternbuch: Recollections Prepared by a Grandchild.* Bnei Brak, Israel: E. Hershowitz, 1994.
Shain, Ruchoma. *All for the Best.* Jerusalem: Feldheim, 1995.
_____. *All for the Boss.* Jerusalem: Feldheim, 1984.
_____. *Dearest Children.* Jerusalem: Feldheim, 1992.
_____. *Reaching the Stars.* Jerusalem: Feldheim, 1990.
_____. *Shining Lights.* Jerusalem: Feldheim, 1997.
Shapiro, Sarah. *Don't You Know It's a Perfect World?* Southfield, Mich.: Targum, 1998.
_____. *Growing with My Children.* Southfield, Mich.: Targum, 1990.
Tenenbaum, S.M. *From My Father's Table: Stories of Warmth and Inspiration.* New York: Mesorah, 1998.
Walburg, Rivka. *A Child Like That.* Jerusalem: Feldheim, 1992.
Wehl, Rabbi Yaakov, and Hadassah. *House Calls to Eternity: The Story of Dr. Selma Wehl, Heroine of Medical Practice and Torah Living.* New York: Mesorah, 1987.

ANTHOLOGIES/COLLECTIONS/JOURNALS

Gergel, Sara. Ed. *Chizuk Lines: Being Organized* Series. Jerusalem.
_____. *Chizuk Lines: Six Stories for Children.* Jerusalem.
_____. *Chizuk Lines Children's Tefilla* Series. 3 Vols. Jerusalem.
_____. *Chizuk Lines Magazine for the Jewish Woman.* 7 Vols. Jerusalem.
Gurary, Tema. Ed. *Aura: A Reader on Jewish Womanhood.* New York: Lubavitch Women's Organization, 1984.
Rubin, Devora. Ed. *Daughters of Destiny: Women Who Revolutionized Jewish Life and Torah Education.* New York: Mesorah, 1988.
Shapiro, Sarah. Ed. *Horizons: The Jewish Family Journal.* Vol. 1, No. 1, 1994. Published quarterly Lazewnik, Libby, and Miriam Zakon. Current Eds. Southfield, Mich.: Targum, 1994.
_____. *More of Our Lives: An Anthology of Jewish Women's Writings.* Southfield, Mich.: Targum, 1993.
_____. *Of Home and Heart: Reflections on the World of the Jewish Woman.* New York: Mesorah, 1993.
_____. *Our Lives: An Anthology of Jewish Women's Writings.* Southfield, Mich.: Targum, 1991.
Shifren, Rivkah. Ed. *Bat Kol: Jewish Women's Journal.* No. 5, 1996. (Premier Israel issue.) Published bimonthly. Vol. 1, No. 1 published in Los Angeles, 1994.
Slonim, Rivkah. Ed. *Total Immersion: A Mikveh Anthology.* Northvale, N.J.: Jason Aronson, 1996.

HOLOCAUST TESTIMONIALS

Banet, Chana Marcus. *They Called Me Frau Anna.* Lakewood, N.J.: CIS, 1990.
Benisch, Pearl. *To Vanquish the Dragon.* Jerusalem: Feldheim, 1991.
Eilenberg, Anna. *Sisters in the Storm.* Lakewood, N.J.: CIS, 1992.
Friedman, Peska, with Fayge Silverman. *Going Forward: A True Story of Courage, Hope and Perseverance.* New York: Mesorah, 1994.
Gabel, Dina. *Behind the Ice Curtain.* Lakewood, N.J.: CIS, 1992.

Gliksman, Devora. *Nor the Moon by Night.* Jerusalem: Feldheim, 1997.
_____. *A Sun and a Shield.* Jerusalem: Feldheim, 1996.
Klein, R.L. *The Scent of Snowflowers.* Jerusalem: Feldheim, 1989.
Pomerantz, Rachel. *Wings above the Flames: Stories of Flight, Escape, and Divine Providence during the Holocaust.* Lakewood, N.J.: CIS, 1992.
Worch, Renee. *Flight: A Jewish Family's Valiant Struggle to Escape Nazi Occupation.* New York: Mesorah, 1988.
_____. *Survival: Inspiring Accounts of Heroes and Heroines of the Holocaust.* New York: Mesorah, 1992.

INFORMATIVE/SELF-HELP

Aiken, Lisa. *To Be a Jewish Woman.* Northvale, N.J.: Jason Aronson, 1992.
Abramov, Tehilla. *The Secret of Jewish Femininity: Insights into the Practice of Taharat HaMishpachah.* Southfield, Mich.: Targum, 1988.
_____. *Straight from the Heart: A Torah Perspective on Mothering through Nursing.* Southfield, Mich.: Targum, 1990.
Abramov, Yirmiyohu, and Tehilla Abramov. *Our Family, Our Strength: Creating a Jewish Home.* Southfield, Mich.: Targum, 1997.
_____. *Two Halves of a Whole: Torah Guidelines for Marriage.* Southfield, Mich.: Targum, 1994.
Adahan, Miriam. *Appreciating People (including Yourself!).* Jerusalem: Feldheim, 1988.
_____. *Awareness: The Key to Acceptance, Forgiveness and Growth.* Jerusalem: Feldheim, 1994.
_____. *EMETT: A Step-by-Step Guide to Maturity Established through Torah.* Jerusalem: Feldheim, 1987.
_____. *It's All a Gift.* Jerusalem: Feldheim, 1992.
_____. *Living with Difficult People (including Yourself).* Jerusalem: Feldheim, 1991.
_____. *The Miriam Adahan Handbook: "Nobody's Perfect": Maintaining Emotional Health.* Southfield, Mich.: Targum, 1994.
_____. *Raising Children to Care: A Jewish Guide to Childrearing.* Jerusalem: Feldheim, 1988.
Berg, Nechama, and Chaya Levine. *It's About Time: The Guide to Successful Homemaking.* New York: Tamar, 1992.
Dansky, Miriam. *Gateshead: Its Community, Its Personalities, Its Institutions.* Southfield, Mich.: Targum, 1992.
Finkelstein, Rabbi Baruch, and R.N. Michal. *B'Sha'ah Tovah: The Jewish Woman's Clinical and Halachic Guide to Pregnancy and Childbirth.* Jerusalem: Feldheim, 1993.
Frankiel, Tamar. *The Voice of Sarah: Feminine Spirituality and Traditional Judaism.* San Francisco: HarperCollins, 1990.
Glaser, Sarah. *Lifesaver! The Jewish Homemaker's Survival Kit.* Southfield, Mich.: Targum, 1996.
Heller, Rebbetzin Tziporah. *More Precious than Pearls: Selected Insights into the Qualities of the Ideal Woman Based on Eshes Chayil.* Jerusalem: Feldheim, 1993.
Kaganoff, Malka. *Dear Kallah: A Practical Guide for the New Bride.* Jerusalem and New York: Feldheim, 1993.

Levi, Miriam. *Effective Jewish Parenting*. Jerusalem: Feldheim, 1986.
_____. *More Effective Jewish Parenting*. New York: Mesorah, 1998.
Manolson, Gila. *Inside Outside*. Southfield, Mich.: Targum, 1997.
_____. *The Magic Touch: A Candid Look at the Jewish Approach to Relationships*. Jerusalem: Har Nof, 1992.
Radcliffe, Sarah Chana. *Aizer K'negdo: The Jewish Woman's Guide to Happiness in Marriage*. Southfield, Mich.: Targum, 1988.
_____. *Akeres Habayis: Realizing Your Potential as a Jewish Homemaker*. Southfield, Mich.: Targum, 1991.
_____. *The Delicate Balance: Love and Authority in Torah Parenting*. Southfield, Mich.: Targum, 1989.
_____. *Smooth Sailing: Navigating Life's Challenges*. Southfield, Mich.: Targum, 1994.
_____. *Teen Esteem*. Southfield, Mich.: Targum, 1992.
Rubinoff, Elaine. *The Art of Teaching: Practical Strategies for Effective Chinuch*. Jerusalem: Feldheim, 1996.
Samet, Yehudis. *The Other Side of the Story: Giving People the Benefit of the Doubt—Stories and Strategies*. New York: Mesorah, 1996.
Shofnos, Chana, and Bat Tova Zwebner. *The Healing Visit: Insights into the Mitzvah of Bikur Cholim*. Southfield, Mich.: Targum, 1989.
Stein, Shani. *The Survival Guide to Shidduchim: Everything You Need to Know About Jewish Dating*. Southfield, Mich.: Targum, 1997.
Weinreich, Roiza D. *In Joy*. New York: Mesorah, 1993.
Zolty, Shoshana Pantel. *"And All Your Children Shall Be Learned": Women and the Study of Torah in Jewish Law and History*. Northvale, N.J.: Jason Aronson, 1993.
Zornberg, Avivah Gottlieb. *Genesis: The Beginning of Desire*. Philadelphia and Jerusalem: Jewish Publication Society, 1995.

Fiction

Anon. *And Rachel Was His Wife*. Marsi Tabak. Ed. Jerusalem: Feldheim, 1990.
Benjamin, Ruth. *All the Hidden Children*. Southfield, Mich.: Targum, 1995.
_____. *On a Golden Chain*. Lakewood, N.J.: CIS, 1991.
_____. *A Stranger to Her People*. Lakewood, N.J.: CIS, 1993.
_____. *Yesterday's Child*. Lakewood, N.J.: CIS, 1992.
Birnhack, Sarah. *Family Secrets*. Southfield, Mich.: Targum, 1993.
_____. *Promise Me Tomorrow*. Lakewood, N.J.: CIS, 1990.
_____. *Search My Heart*. New York: Moznaim, 1986.
Chasen, Estelle. *Chava's Story*. Jerusalem: Feldheim, 1997.
Firestone, Beth. *Candles in My Window*. Southfield, Mich.: Targum, 1990.
Halpern, Chaiky. *The House on Kyverdale Road*. Jerusalem: Feldheim, 1995.
Lamet, Rosalie. *City of Diamonds*. Southfield, Mich.: Targum, 1996.
Lazewnik, Libby. *Between the Thorns*. Southfield, Mich.: Targum, 1994.
_____. *Give Me the Moon*. Southfield, Mich.: Targum, 1996.
_____. *Secret Accounts*. New York: Shaar, 1997.

Lepon, Shoshana. *No Greater Treasure: Stories of Extraordinary Women Drawn from the Talmud and Midrash.* Southfield, Mich.: Targum, 1990.

Meyer, Henye. *The Exiles of Crocodile Island.* New York: Mesorah, 1984.

Pearlman, Ruthie. *Getting It Right.* Princeton, N.J.: Bristol, Rhein and Englander, 1991.

_____. *Making It Last.* Princeton, N.J.: Bristol, Rhein and Englander, 1991.

_____. *Working It Out.* Princeton, N.J.: Bristol, Rhein and Englander, 1990.

Peterseil, Tehila. *The Safe Place.* New York and Jerusalem: Pitspopany, 1996.

Pomerantz, Rachel. *Cactus Blossoms.* Southfield, Mich.: Targum, 1997.

_____. *A Time to Rend, a Time to Sew.* Jerusalem: Feldheim, 1996.

_____. *Wildflower.* Princeton, N.J.: Bristol, Rhein and Englander, 1989.

Rubin, Chana Stavsky. *A Time to Live.* Lakewood, N.J.: CIS, 1988.

_____. *Tomorrow May Be Too Late.* New York: Tamar, 1995.

Schiff, Rena. *My Special Brother.* Lakewood, N.J.: CIS, 1991.

Schleimer, Sarah. *Far from the Place We Called Home.* Jerusalem: Feldheim, 1994.

Spitzer, Lena. *My Rock and My Redeemer.* Southfield, Mich.: Targum, 1993.

Vogiel, Eva. *One Tiny Spark.* Lakewood, N.J.: CIS, 1989.

Waysman, Dvora. *The Pomegranate Pendant: A Historical Novel.* Jerusalem: Feldheim, 1995.

Zakon, Miriam, and Libby Lazewnik. Eds. *Fiction: Twenty Contemporary Jewish Stories.* Southfield, Mich.: Targum, 1993.

SECONDARY SOURCES

Adelman, Penina V. *Miriam's Well: Rituals for Jewish Women around the Year.* Fresh Meadows, N.Y.: Biblio Press, 1986.

Appelman, Solomon. *The Jewish Woman in Judaism: The Significance of Woman's Status in Religious Culture.* Hicksville, N.Y.: Exposition, 1979.

Baker, Adrienne. *The Jewish Woman in Contemporary Society: Transitions and Traditions.* Washington Square, N.Y.: New York University Press, 1993.

Beaujour, Michel. *Poetics of the Literary Self-Portrait.* Trans. Yara Milos. New York and London: New York University Press, 1991.

Ben Reuven, Yisrael. *Male and Female He Created Them: A Guide to Classical Torah Commentary on the Roles and Natures of Men and Women.* Southfield, Mich.: Targum, 1996.

Biale, Rachel. *Women and Jewish Law: An Exploration of Women's Issues in Halakhic Sources.* New York: Schocken, 1984.

Boyarin, Jonathan, and Daniel Boyarin. Eds. *Jews and Other Differences: The New Jewish Cultural Studies.* Minneapolis and London: University of Minnesota Press, 1997.

Brayer, Menachem M. *The Jewish Woman in Rabbinic Literature: A Psychohistorical Perspective.* Hoboken, N.J.: Ktav, 1986.

_____. *The Jewish Woman in Rabbinic Literature: A Psychosocial Perspective.* Hoboken, N.J.: Ktav, 1986.

Brodzki, Bella, and Celeste Schenck. Eds. *Life/Lines: Theorizing Women's Autobiography.* Ithaca, N.Y., and London: Cornell University Press, 1988.

Butler, Judith. *Gender Trouble: Feminism and the Subversion of Identity.* New York: Routledge, 1989.

De Saussure, Ferdinand. "Nature of the Linguistic Sign." From *Course in General Linguistics*. Trans. Wade Baskins. In *Critical Theory since Plato*. Rev. Ed. Hazard Adams. Ed. Fort Worth, Tex.: Harcourt Brace Jovanovich, 1992.

Eibeshitz, Jehoshua, and Anna Eilenberg-Eibeshitz. Eds. and Trans. *Women in the Holocaust: A Collection of Testimonies*. Vol. 1. New York: Remember, 1993.

_____. *Women in the Holocaust: A Collection of Testimonies*. Vol. 2. New York: Remember, 1994.

Ellison, Rabbi Getsel. *Woman and the Mitzvot. Vol. 1: Serving the Creator: A Guide to the Rabbinic Sources*. English version prepared by Rabbi Mendell Lewittes and Avner Tomaschoff. Jerusalem: World Zionist Organization, 1986.

Epstein, Cynthia F. *Deceptive Distinctions: Theory and Research on Sex, Gender and the Social Order*. New Haven, Conn.: Yale University Press, 1988.

Farganis, Sondra. *Situating Feminism: From Thought to Action*. Thousand Oaks, Calif.: SAGE, Inc., 1994.

Furman, Nelly. "Textual Feminism." In *Women and Language in Literature and Society*. Ruth Borker, Sally McConnell-Ginet and Nelly Furman. Eds. New York: Praeger, 1980.

Fuss, Diana. *Essentially Speaking: Feminism, Nature and Difference*. New York and London: Routledge, 1989.

Gilbert, Sandra M., and Susan Gubar. *The Madwoman in the Attic*. New Haven, Conn., and London: Yale University Press, 1979.

Gilligan, Carol. "Hearing the Difference: Theorizing Connection." In *Hypatia*. Spring 1995.

_____. *In a Different Voice: Psychological Theory and Women's Development*. Cambridge, Mass.: Harvard University Press, 1982.

Goldenberg, Myrna. "Holocaust Literature: The Burden of Gender." An unpublished paper prepared in June 1995.

Goldstein, Elyse. "Taking Back the Waters." In *Lilith*. Summer 1986.

Gordon, Suzanne. *Prisoner of Men's Dreams*. Boston: Little, Brown, 1991.

Grant, Linda. "The Supermarket of Gender Politics: Men v. Women in the 1990s." In *The Jewish Quarterly*. Spring 1997.

Greenberg, Blu. *On Women and Judaism: A View from Tradition*. Philadelphia: Jewish Publication Society of America, 1981.

Halkin, Hillel. "Feminizing Jewish Studies." In *Commentary*. February 1998.

Halpern, Micah D., and Chana Safrai. Eds. *Jewish Legal Writings by Women*. Jerusalem: Urim, 1998.

Hauptman, Judith. *Rereading the Rabbis: A Woman's Voice*. Boulder, Colo.: Westview, 1998.

Heilbrun, Carolyn G. *Writing a Woman's Life*. New York and London: W.W. Norton, 1988.

Hekman, Susan J. *Moral Voices, Moral Selves: Carol Gilligan and Feminist Moral Theory*. University Park, Pa.: Pennsylvania State University Press, 1995.

Henry, Sondra, and Emily Taitz. *Written Out of History: Our Jewish Foremothers*. Fourth Ed. New York: Biblio Press, 1990.

Hubbard, Ruth, and Marian Lowe. Eds. *Woman's Nature: Rationalizations of Inequality*. New York: Pergamon, 1984.

Kaufman, Debra Renee. *Rachel's Daughters: Newly Orthodox Jewish Women*. New Brunswick and London: Rutgers University Press, 1991.

Kaufman, Michael. *Feminism and Judaism: Women, Tradition, and the Women's Movement*. Jerusalem: Heritage, 1996.

_____. *The Woman in Jewish Law and Tradition*. Northvale, N.J., and London: Jason Aronson, 1993.

Koltun, Elizabeth. Ed. *Jewish Woman: New Perspectives*. New York: Schocken, 1975.

Lanser, Susan Sniader. *Fictions of Authority: Women Writers and Narrative Voice*. Ithaca, N.Y., and London: Cornell University Press, 1992.

Levi, Leo. *Modern Liberation: A Torah Perspective on Contemporary Lifestyles*. Brooklyn, N.Y.: Hemed, 1998.

Meiselman, Moshe. *Jewish Woman in Jewish Law*. New York: Ktav, 1978.

Miller, Yisroel. *In Search of the Jewish Woman: A Torah Journey*. Jerusalem: Feldheim, 1984.

Ostriker, Alicia. "The Nerves of a Midwife: Contemporary American Women's Poetry." From *Parnassus: Poetry in Review*. Repr. in *The Pushcart Prize IV: Best of the Small Presses*. Bill Henderson. Ed. New York: Avon, 1979.

Peskowitz, Miriam, and Laura Levitt. Eds. *Judaism since Gender*. New York: Routledge, 1997.

Plaskow, Judith. *Standing Again at Sinai: Judaism from a Feminist Perspective*. New York: HarperCollins, 1991.

Powers, Elizabeth. "A Farewell to Feminism." In *Commentary*. January 1997.

Powers, Meredith A. *The Heroine in Western Literature: The Archetype and Her Reemergence in Modern Prose*. Jefferson, N.C., and London: McFarland, 1991.

Ringelheim, Joan. "Gender and Genocide: A Split Memory." A paper prepared for presentation at the Conference on Women in the Holocaust, Jerusalem, June 19–22, 1995.

Rittner, Carol, and John K. Roth. Eds. *Different Voices: Women and the Holocaust*. New York: Paragon, 1993.

Rosenfeld, Alvin H. *A Double Dying: Reflections on Holocaust Literature*. Bloomington, Ind., and London: Indiana University Press, 1980.

Sacks, Maurie. Ed. *Active Voices: Women in Jewish Culture*. Urbana and Chicago, Ill.: University of Illinois Press, 1995.

Schneider, Susan Weidman. Ed. *Jewish and Female: A Guide and Sourcebook for Today's Jewish Woman*. New York: Simon and Schuster, 1985.

Schor, Naomi, and Elizabeth Weed. Eds. *The Essential Difference*. Bloomington and Indianapolis: Indiana University Press, 1994.

Schweickart, Patrocinio. "Reading Ourselves: Toward a Feminist Theory of Reading." In *Contemporary Literary Criticism: Literary and Cultural Studies*. Third Ed. Robert Con Davis and Ronald Schleifer. Eds. New York and London: Longman, 1994.

Showalter, Elaine. "Feminist Criticism in the Wilderness." In *Contemporary Literary Criticism: Literary and Cultural Studies*. Third Ed. Robert Con Davis and Ronald Schleifer. Eds. New York and London: Longman, 1994.

Spelman, Elizabeth V. *Inessential Woman. Problems of Exclusion in Feminist Thought*. Boston: Beacon, 1988.

Telushkin, Rabbi Joseph. *Jewish Literacy: The Most Important Things to Know about the Jewish Religion, Its People, and Its History*. New York: William Morrow, 1991.

Wandor, Michelene. "The Sex Divide in Jewish Culture: A Meditation on Jewishness and Gender." In *The Jewish Quarterly.* Spring 1997.

Wellsprings: A Quarterly Journal Exploring the Inner Dimensions of Torah and Jewish Life. New York: Lubavitch Youth Organization.

Wolowelsky, Joel B. *Women, Jewish Law, and Modernity: New Opportunities in a Post-Feminist Age.* Hoboken, N.J.: Ktav, 1997.

Index

OHIO UNIVERSITY LIBRARY

Please return this book as soon as you have finished with it. In order to avoid a fine it must be returned by the latest date stamped below. All books are subject to recall after two weeks or immediately if needed for reserve.

DEC 0 7 2000

NOV _ 2 2000

CF